Charles Seale-Hayne Library
University of Plymouth
(01752) 588 588
LibraryandITenquiries@plymouth.ac.uk

Digital information

Order or anarchy?

Digital information

Order or anarchy?

edited by
Hazel Woodward and **Lorraine Estelle**

 facet publishing

Published by Facet Publishing,
7 Ridgmount Street, London WC1E 7AE
www.facetpublishing.co.uk

Facet Publishing is wholly owned by CILIP: the Chartered Institute of Library
and Information Professionals.

British Library Cataloguing in Publication Data
A catalogue record for this book is available from the British Library.

ISBN 978-1-85604-680-0
First published 2010

Text printed on FSC accredited material.

Mixed Sources
Product group from well-managed
forests and other controlled sources
www.fsc.org Cert no. SA-COC-1565
© 1996 Forest Stewardship Council

Typeset from editors' files by Facet Publishing in 12/14 pt American Garamond
and Nimbus Sans.
Printed and made in Great Britain by MPG Books Group, UK.

Contents

Acknowledgements

The authors are deeply indebted to Fytton Rowland – Hazel's husband – for all his assistance in proofing and sub-editing this book and, of course, for all the support he gave and cups of tea he made while we were working on it. Not to mention walking Freddy – Lorraine's dog (when he's really a cat person). Lorraine would like to thank Laurie for being so supportive. And finally we have to thank Darran Rowe who works in the Kings Norton Library at Cranfield University for valiantly trying to rescue lost files of manuscripts which had vanished into cyberspace. Aptly, a peril of our digital world.

Hazel Woodward
Lorraine Estelle

Contributors

Rick Anderson is Associate Director for Scholarly Resources and Collections at the University of Utah's Marriott Library. He earned his BS and MLIS degrees at Brigham Young University, and has worked previously as a bibliographer for YBP, Inc., as Head Acquisitions Librarian for the University of North Carolina, Greensboro, and as Director of Resource Acquisition at the University of Nevada, Reno. He serves on numerous editorial and advisory boards and writes a regular op-ed column for *Against the Grain* entitled 'In My Humble (But Correct) Opinion'. His book, *Buying and Contracting for Resources and Services: a how-to-do-it manual for librarians*, was published in 2004 by Neal-Schuman, Inc. In 2005 Rick was identified by *Library Journal* as a 'Mover & Shaker' – one of the '50 people shaping the future of libraries'. In 2008 he was elected President of the North American Serials Interest Group, and he was named an Association of Research Libraries (ARL) Research Library Leadership Fellow for 2009–10. He is a popular speaker on subjects related to the future of scholarly information and information services in higher education.

Alastair Dunning is Digitization Programme Manager at the Joint Information Systems Committee (JISC), which provides support for the use of ICT in higher and further education in the UK. Alastair's role is overseeing the successful completion of over 50 digitization projects funded by JISC (www.jisc.ac.uk/digitisation), many of which are now freely available on the internet. He also oversees various other strands of work, including transatlantic digitization programmes and work to embed digitized content in various JISC-funded portals. Alastair's professional concerns involve fighting the hydra of non-interoperability, slaying the dragon of digital apathy and uncovering the elixir of sustainability.

Lorraine Estelle is Chief Executive of JISC Collections, the organization that manages the procurement and licensing of a broad array of intellectual property for academic libraries. JISC Collections collaborates with its library members and the publishing community to undertake research that drives the development of licensing and business models in line with user needs, innovative technology and the future of digital content. Recent projects in this area have included the National E-books Observatory and E-books for FE. She is a member of the Knowledge Exchange Licensing Group, which looks at the issues of digital licensing and procurement at multinational level, and she is an active participant in the ICOLC conferences. She is a member of the EDINA Management Board, the chair of the ETHOS Governance Steering Committee and until recently was a member of the Royal Society of Chemistry Publishing Board. Prior to joining JISC Collections she worked in the publishing industry, firstly in trade book publishing and then in the area of children's educational books and multimedia.

Wilma Mossink is the legal advisor of SURFfoundation/SURFdiensten. Her expertise is in the areas of copyright management in higher education and the legal aspects of making content and information openly available.

Wilma also advises the legal committee of the FOBID, the Dutch Library Forum. In this capacity, she represents the Netherlands in the Expert Group on Information Law of EBLIDA, the European organization for libraries, and she is the Dutch representative on the Copyright and Other Legal Matters committee of IFLA (CLM). She is a member of several national and international working groups, including the National Information Standards Organization (NISO) ONIX-PL Working Group and the Knowledge Exchange Licensing working group.

Ian Russell is Chief Executive of the Association of Learned and Professional Society Publishers (ALPSP), the world's largest international association for scholarly and professional publishers. His interest in publishing began at age 15, when he contributed a regular feature to the British Association for Young Scientists magazine *Scope*. He studied physics with astronomy at Southampton University (UK) and then undertook a vocational graduate management training scheme before starting a career in academic publishing in 1992 with Institute of Physics Publishing (IOPP), rising to become Assistant Director, Journals, where he had responsibility for the editorial content of IOPP's 40-plus journals.

In 2004 Ian became the youngest ever Head of Publishing at The Royal Society – the UK's national academy of sciences and the publisher of the world's oldest journal – and joined ALPSP in October 2006.

He is a Director of the Copyright Licensing Agency, Portland Press Ltd and the Publishers' Licensing Society. He is also a trustee and board member of the International Network for the Availability of Scientific Publications (INASP) and a member of the Board of JISC.

Colin Steele is Emeritus Fellow of the Australian National University (ANU). Previously, he was Director of Scholarly Information Strategies (2002–2003); University Librarian ANU (1980–2002); Deputy Librarian ANU (1976–1980); and Assistant Librarian at the Bodleian Library, Oxford (1967–1976).

Colin is the Convenor of the National Scholarly Communications Forum and author/editor of seven books, as well as over 300 articles and reviews. He is a regular reviewer for, and on the Board of, several international journals. In 1998 he was awarded a Fellowship by both the British and Australian Library Associations, only the sixth double Fellowship in history. In 2001 he was elected an Honorary Fellow of the Australian Academy of Humanities and in 2002 he received the Australian Centenary Medal for scholarly communication services.

Graham Stone has been working with e-resources for over 15 years. He is currently Electronic Resources Manager and Repository Administrator at the University of Huddersfield (UK), and has previously held posts at the University of Bolton and Manchester Metropolitan University. A member of the UK Serials Group (UKSG) Committee since 2001, Graham is UKSG Secretary and a member of the *Serials* editorial board. He is editor-in-chief of *E-Resources Management Handbook*.

Hazel Woodward currently works for Cranfield University – the UK's only postgraduate university – as University Librarian and Director of Cranfield Press. Prior to her job at Cranfield she was Head of Electronic

Information at Loughborough University. Hazel also studied for her PhD – on the topic of scholarly communication and libraries – at Loughborough University, and she has subsequently been involved in library and information research projects on various aspects of digital information resources over the years, including the JISC National E-books Observatory project, and MAGIC, which examined access to, and management of, grey literature. Her first edited book *The International Serials Industry*, was published in 1993 and she has published widely in the book and journal literature. Presenting papers at conferences, both nationally and internationally, has given Hazel the opportunity to travel to many exotic (and some not-so-exotic) locations including India, China and the USA. She has also been very active on the professional front, participating in and chairing committees for JISC, Sconul, UKSG, ICOLC and COUNTER. She is currently on the board of directors for both JISC Collections and COUNTER, chairs the JISC Journals Working Group and is a member of the JISC E-books Working Group. She is co-editor of the UKSG journal *Serials* and a Visiting Professor at University College London. In 2009 Hazel was awarded an MBE for services to higher education

Preface

We are delighted to have been given the opportunity of editing this book on the theme of 'Digital Information: order or anarchy?'. In the early stages of preparation, when discussing the outline and selecting the contributors, we were anxious to ensure that we covered all the major aspects of the digital revolution that is taking place across our industry. Thus we not only chose contributors from a number of different countries to ensure the widest possible perspective, but we were also keen to include publishers, non-traditional information workers, and even a lawyer, in pursuit of our goal.

The theme of order and anarchy permeates the chapters. As editors we were intrigued by the possibilities (and uncertainties) of future developments in our digital universe and we wished to explore the potential impact on libraries, publishing companies and all the other players in the marketplace. Will the present relatively orderly system of scholarly communication survive into the future or will the possibilities that technology affords, create disruption and anarchy? And what is being done today that will help an orderly transfer to the future?

The chapters by Rick Anderson, Colin Steele and Ian Russell essentially focus on the process and evolution of scholarly communication in the digital age from their own individual perspectives. Anderson identifies three 'crunch points' for libraries and publishers: searching and finding information; library collections; and pricing. In a world where Google has effectively taken over the document-finding role from libraries, there is one area that it has not yet fully invaded (but is making some progress). That is the role of third-party broker for expensive high quality documents such as scholarly journals and monographs. But how will libraries respond as more and more scholarly material becomes easily searchable and increasingly freely available on the internet? The final crunch point is pricing and business models – a dilemma that many would maintain that has been around for decades. Anderson works through various future scenarios around these topics and points to essential mission change for academic and research libraries.

Colin Steele focuses on e-books and scholarly communication futures. Technology is creating many opportunities for book publishers in terms of dissemination – witness the development of new e-book services, e-book readers, print-on-demand publication and the Espresso Book Machine. Authors too can utilize new methods of textual output and share their content through both formal and informal social networking services. However, Steele contends that we are currently confronted by a situation in which the mechanisms for the digital distribution of academic monographs are increasing, yet academic conservatism and research evaluation standards negate e-publication. What we are still searching for is an infrastructure for the digital world untrammelled by historical legacies of the print world.

'For the future of digital information to be orderly, that information must be discoverable, accessible, structured, interoperable, linked, semantically tagged and well identified; it must have clear provenance and good version control; and it must be preserved and curated.' These are the opening words from our publisher contributor, Ian Russell, who goes on to examine how publishers might ensure that we have an orderly progression to a digital future by paying attention to these issues. He also examines the issues, addressed by Anderson, of discoverability and pricing from a publisher's perspective. He concludes with four future publishing scenarios – one of which he believes will result in chaos.

Technological advances mean that non-traditional players can now create and disseminate digital information. Libraries are now publishers, and companies such as Google and Microsoft are undertaking mass digitization projects. Alastair Dunning's chapter, 'Digitizing the Past', describes how public sector funding has resulted in the digitization of some amazing collections. For example, Darwin Online provides a single source of all Darwin's published and unpublished writings and Old Bailey Online makes fully searchable court proceedings from 1674 to 1912. Perhaps one of the most exciting projects described in the chapter is the Great War Archive, which contains over 6500 items contributed by the general public. Every item originates from, or relates to, someone's experience of World War 1. This project has made available to scholars material that was previously stored by private individuals, and illustrates how the use of amateur digitization can bring together collections of previously unknown material.

However, there are dangers, particularly long term, that some digital collections will not be there for the scholar of the future. Although significant capital funding has enabled the creation of these collections, the ongoing funding streams for maintenance and web delivery are not always available. Their sustainability is also threatened because some content is little used. To ensure higher use, open and multiple standards must be applied, in order that the content can be found both by machines and by individuals. The public sector needs not only to rely on public funding but also to develop strategic business models to ensure sustainability.

Issues around intellectual property rights challenge not only the traditional publishers but also the new players. In their chapter, Wilma Mossink and Lorraine Estelle describe the problems, and some of the work that is currently being undertaken to address them. The power of the internet means that it has never been easier to create and access content, and perhaps more importantly to reuse and 'mash-up' a number of content sources. However, the existing copyright regime is not designed for such technological opportunities. For example, current law is not designed with mass digitization projects in mind. These projects involve digitization of high volumes, and, although cultural interest is high, there is little commercial value. Currently, much expense and many hours are involved in tracing authors who are not easily identifiable. Sometimes the risks are too high, and valuable content is not digitized because of fears of copyright infringement. A careful balance is needed to ensure order rather than anarchy. The rights of authors and their publishers need to be protected to ensure vibrant and economically sustainable creative industries. At the same time, policy needs to change, especially for the educational sector, to ensure innovative use of content and the creation of new knowledge.

The users of digital content should be able to navigate a well ordered information environment without unreasonable barriers, and to find the information they seek. However, as Graham Stone points out in his chapter on resource discovery, the landscape is messy and libraries face enormous challenges in the digital marketplace. The user is not always persuaded to start their search for information by using library resources. Library OPACs are often limited by a structure based on print rather than digital concepts. Content is delivered from silos and users have to navigate multiple systems, often requiring separate authentication. Federated search is a solution, but perhaps one that does not yet provide the easy one-stop-shop approach that meets user expectations. This applies especially to the young, who are used to dynamic, personalized and increasingly mobile experiences such as those delivered by Facebook and Amazon. Libraries and publishers need to respond urgently to the changing needs of scholars and other users who 'search for information' on the internet rather than consulting print formats such as the journal or the monograph.

The chapters in this book focus mainly on the academic perspective. However, the issues tackled are pertinent to the broader information industry, including trade publishers, bookshops, public libraries and national libraries. The editors' opening chapter provides an overview of the digital revolution and its impact on all of these sectors. We live in a period of rapid change, which provides for many opportunities but which also threatens the status quo. To quote Darwin: 'It is not the strongest species that survive, nor the most intelligent, but the ones most responsive to change.'

While this book does not present a definitive answer to the many challenges faced by the information industry, we hope that it looks to the future. In order to prevent a decline into anarchy we need to be diligent in ensuring that new initiatives and technologies conform to the standards that harness technology, and which improve access to information to the scholar and the general public. In effect, change must enable the democratization of information.

Hazel Woodward
Lorraine Estelle

1

Introduction: digital information, an overview of the landscape

Lorraine Estelle and Hazel Woodward

As seasoned information professionals it is easy to think that we have a reasonable understanding of the way in which the world of information and associated technologies is moving. However, the world is changing fast and many of our core beliefs and understandings will, without doubt, be impacted by these changes. In the words of Clifford Lynch:

> Digital technologies have opened the door to a host of new possibilities for sharing knowledge and generated entirely new forms of content that must be made broadly available.   (ARL, 2009)

Take, for example, the way in which users search for information. Only a few years ago, librarians would advise that the starting point for all literature searches should be an abstracting and indexing (A&I) service, or a reference publication such as a handbook or encyclopedia. While this advice is still given in appropriate circumstances, all librarians know that everyone (ourselves included) uses an internet search engine such as Google, Google Scholar or Yahoo! as a first port of call. We know this by talking to, and observing, our users, and recent research by the Centre for Information Behaviour and the Evaluation of Research (CIBER, 2008) has validated it.

In 2009 the UK Serials Group (UKSG) ran a student competition. Entrants were asked to write a short submission on how they used libraries, electronic resources and the internet; the winner was then invited to run a workshop at the 2009 UKSG conference. The winner was Claire Duddy, and her workshop was a runaway success. Duddy wrote in a subsequent article for *Serials*:

> As a librarian (in-waiting) even the idea of a 'quick and dirty' search with Google is an illicit thrill. It is almost too easy: shouldn't there be some effort involved in finding useful, valid information? And if librarians use Google, aren't we just undermining ourselves? It is a difficult thing then to admit: Google is my first stop for all my information needs, whether I am researching my dinner or my dissertation.

However, she went on to say:

> Librarians who accept the importance of Google in their users' academic lives are easier for users to relate to. They can also help to encourage research that takes in a wide variety of sources and types of information. We can promote internet searching and Google alongside more traditional literature searching and A&I databases; the use of a wide range of searching skills and information sources can be encouraged and developed . . . the choice is not between Google and libraries. Both have their strengths and weaknesses. (Duddy, 2009)

We should be reassured that while Duddy does indeed start with Google, she then goes on to utilize more specialist information retrieval tools. However, there are clearly many students who do not. Professor Tara Brabazon from Brighton University has coined the phrase 'Google is white bread for the mind':

> Google offers easy answers to difficult questions. But students do not know how to tell if they come from serious refereed work or are merely composed of shallow ideas, superficial surfing and fleeting commitment. (Frean, 2008)

Brabazon is undoubtedly correct. However, there is another important factor when considering the effectiveness of a Google search – and the figures are staggering. Williams estimates that 'the surface web is about 177 terabytes while the total web is about 91,000 terabytes, so the total web has 500 times more content than is openly accessible' (Williams, 2009).

It is arguable that many people are simply unaware that there is content available on what is known as the 'invisible web' or 'deep web'. The invisible web contains the content not surfaced by the search engines, content that is often only accessible on payment of a toll or subscription fee. Even those who are aware of the invisible web, and who have access to subscription content through an affiliation to a library, are unlikely to start their search there. Google is ubiquitous and, indeed, the use of Google is so popular that 'to Google' is now a verb, and entered the *Oxford English Dictionary* in 2006. This means that information professionals have a huge task in helping users to find and use the content on the invisible web. It is a core belief of the information professional that access to high-quality information is at the heart of research and the knowledge economy. Graham Stone, in Chapter 6, further examines the complexities and challenges of resource discovery in the digital era and asks what the future holds for libraries and librarians.

The academic library of the future

There is little doubt that the role of the academic library is changing in the digital age. A recent feature on the future of libraries in the *Guardian* newspaper stated: 'Academic libraries are changing faster than at any time in their history. Information technology, online databases and catalogues and digitised archives have put the library back at the heart of teaching and learning and academic research on campus' (JISC, 2009).

Such media attention is welcome and raises the profile of libraries. Over the last decade huge strides have been made in the provision of and access to information by libraries. Most major journal publishers now provide their entire portfolio in digital format and the transition by libraries from printed journal holdings to electronic journals (e-journals) is rapid. The traditional journal package as we know it is also evolving. Blogs and wikis, links to research data, RSS feeds and online peer review are all becoming commonplace. Book publishers are catching up, and electronic books (e-books) are becoming an important element of library collections. Scholarly book publishers increasingly publish both print and electronic versions of their books, although this does not generally apply to textbooks. Amazon – a major player in the mass book market – is rapidly signing deals with publishers to make e-books available and providing access to readers via its Kindle e-book reader. If we also consider the huge amounts of older and rarer research materials being made available online by local and national digitization initiatives, the vast scale of the rich information resource available to scholars and researchers becomes apparent.

Our digital heritage

In Chapter 5 Alastair Dunning examines the many issues and technological challenges surrounding the digitization of library heritage collections. There is little doubt that a major future role for academic (and other) libraries will be to disseminate the world's heritage literature and artefacts to a wider audience than just scholars and researchers. However, we must recognize that we do have powerful competition in the form of Google. Google's mission is 'to organise the world's information and make it universally accessible and useful', and it has many millions of dollars to devote to the cause. The Google digitization programme is already well under way, digitizing out-of-copyright books in scores of major research libraries around the world. Dr Rolf Griebel of the Bavarian State Library, a partner in the programme, commented on his library's participation:

> With today's announcement we are opening our library to the world
> and bringing the true purpose of libraries – the discovery of books and
> knowledge – a decisive step further into the digital era. This is an
> exciting effort to help readers around the world discover and access
> Germany's rich literary tradition online – whenever and wherever they
> want.   (Google, 2009)

But Google is not the only show in town. Libraries are also involved in significant digitization programmes and it is heartening to see the extent of national commitment to the provision of digital information. In the USA, the Library of Congress is leading a nationwide digitization effort to scan ageing brittle books – some of which are often too fragile to be handled by researchers – and make them freely available. The programme is sponsored by a $2 million grant from the Alfred P. Sloan Foundation and it involves over 100 libraries, universities and cultural organizations (Library of Congress, 2009). In Europe another initiative is under way: the European Digital Library – Europeana – is aiming to link users directly to digitized heritage content accessible in a Web 2.0 environment. It hopes to expose national content to new audiences and all levels of learning, and extend the knowledge and understanding of each nation's heritage (EDL Foundation, 2007). In the UK, JISC has funded a £22 million digitization programme, which has run in two phases. The first phase saw collections such as the British Library Archival Sound Recordings and British Newspapers 1800–1900 digitized. In the second phase Historic Polar Images, Radio News Archive and the British Cartoon Archive, among others, were made freely available online (Sykes, 2008).

As Alastair Dunning points out in Chapter 5, many challenges remain to be addressed in terms of sustainability of digital collections and application of international standards, but the message for libraries and publishers is clear. The way forward is to continue the digitization of our valuable heritage materials, and also to work towards improving the flow of digital content into wider arenas and allowing users to interact with the digital data.

E-journals, e-books and other e-stuff
E-journals
Journals have always been one of the most important types of resource for scholars. They have also constituted the major spend on materials in most academic libraries. Currently there are about 21,000 peer-reviewed journals published worldwide, containing about 1.4 million articles each year, and the world market for scholarly journals is estimated at £5 billion. According to Mabe (2006), the number of journals continues to grow year on year by about 3% and the number of articles grows at approximately 3.5% per year. Amazingly, these figures have been relatively consistent over the last 200 years. However, that may be about to change. Robert Parker, Managing Director of Royal Society of Chemistry (RSC) Publications, recently told members of his Library Advisory Board that submissions to the RSC are up 47% in 2009. The society published 35% more articles in 2008 and it will publish 30% more again in 2009. Ian Russell, in Chapter 3, goes into more detail regarding the growth of research output. The increasing

output from China and India is already challenging publishers. Russell says: 'We can expect a truly dramatic increase in the quantity, quality and impact of Chinese research. Many observers believe that India is around five years behind China.'

But the ever increasing output of scholarly journals and articles has created, and will continue to create, a major problem for libraries. The so-called 'serials crisis' – the inability of library budgets to keep up with the proliferation of published journals – has been an enduring topic in the library literature for many decades.

Librarians and publishers do need to find a solution to the current dilemma. It is important to the survival of both parties that scholars continue to have access to the research literature. At a strategic level, academic institutions should also be concerned. A recent research report from the UK's Research Information Network (RIN, 2009) shows that even at the current level of spend, e-journals represent good value for money. Users in UK universities downloaded some 102 million articles in 2006–7, at an average cost of 80 pence per article. However, even more importantly, the spend and the use of e-journals in an academic institution correlate with research outcomes. The research found that per capita expenditure and use of e-journals is strongly and positively correlated with the number of papers published, the number of PhD awards and the number of successful research grants awarded to an institution. Given that funding bodies worldwide use such metrics to establish institutional funding levels, vice-chancellors do need to take heed. It is up to librarians to ensure that their voices are heard by higher authorities, and this will continue to be an important role for library consortia and library professional bodies at a national and international level.

There is however, another possible solution.

Open Access

While libraries have traditionally focused on the purchase of journals, the electronic environment has opened up new possibilities. Electronic publishing offers authors the possibility of making their publications freely available on the internet. This is known as Open Access (OA) and it is gaining momentum among both librarians and authors.

There are a number of OA models. Harnad (a major protagonist of OA) identifies two types – 'green' and 'gold' (Harnad et al., 2004). In gold OA the publisher makes the entire e-journal available on the internet free of charge – finding revenue streams from sources other than library subscriptions (e.g. library membership fees or payments from authors). In green OA an article is published in a conventional, subscription-based journal, but the author subsequently makes it available online, via either personal or institutional web pages or in a repository.

The growth of repositories is a worldwide phenomenon. Many academic institutions around the globe now have their own institutional repositories (IR), which contain the research output of their scholars and researchers, including journal articles, book chapters, theses and research reports. Providing that the IR complies with the Open Archives Initiative Protocol for Metadata Harvesting (OAI-PMH), the publications can be discovered by anyone using a generic web search engine (e.g. Google, Yahoo!). In many institutions it is the responsibility of the library to manage and populate the IR, which means that generally the library bears the cost of the 'publishing' activity – particularly in terms of staff costs. There are also a number of international discipline-based repositories, the best known being arXiv[1] for physics and PubMed Central[2] for biomedical sciences.

If OA publishing continues to grow, the impact on publishers and libraries will be considerable. There could come a time when libraries decide to cancel journal subscriptions because a significant proportion of articles published are freely available online. Indeed, research by Norris, Oppenheim and Rowland (2008) shows that in some subject disciplines well over 50% of all published papers *are* already freely available. But whether it is traditional publishers or librarians via their IR who publish materials, there is still a cost associated with the publishing and someone will need to foot the bill.

The future of the journal

Having examined some of the issues surrounding the publishing and provision of journals in the digital environment, it is perhaps time to ask whether the journal, as we know it, is fit for purpose. Already it is apparent that there is no longer a necessity for every library in the UK to retain printed back-files of journals and older books. The UK Research Reserve Project is working on a national UK store, based in the British Library, which will hold journals no longer required by higher education libraries, retain them permanently and make them available to researchers.[3]

Library space is an important issue, which is under scrutiny in many academic institutions. Storage space for printed books and journals is expensive, and more and more space is required year on year. Some institutions see the opportunity for returning freed-up space to lecture rooms and laboratories, others have decided to retain it within the library and create more social, exploratory and group learning space – for example, the Learning Grid at Warwick University (Edwards, 2006).

As libraries continue to remove bound back-volumes of journals from their stacks, what of the current issues of journals that now are predominantly available as e-journals? Will the current system of journal publishing survive? Journals themselves are merely the wrappers for articles, and as publishers increasingly encourage users to access their titles from their own platforms, surely these are looking more and more like databases of articles. The fact that the article metadata is also being released to search engines so that they can be discovered more easily also means that the unit of transaction is becoming the article – not the journal. Publishers, journals editors and possibly some academics would argue that it is the journal title which provides the prestige of a publication.

For decades academia has been obsessed with methods of calculating the quality of journals such as citation rankings and impact factors. These methodologies provide the basis for measuring the research excellence of academic institutions in many countries. If we were to move away from the concept of the journal as the package, how would quality be measured? This issue is already being addressed by the Public Library of Science (PLoS). It is devising an article-level metric for its journals, based predominantly on usage (Binfield, 2009).

However, many publishers are moving into the Web 2.0 space, and more and more journals are providing RSS feeds, blogs and wikis – and even links to background research data – for their authors and readers. Is this a last-ditch attempt to create reader loyalty to the title? Or is it that the journal really is an efficient way of disseminating peer-reviewed information and data? Ian Russell in Chapter 3 clearly thinks it is. Rick Anderson in Chapter 2 is not so sure.

But one thing is certain: the scholarly journal industry has evolved over a long period of time; alongside libraries it has become the custodian of quality control, and industry standards have been developed to ensure discovery, access and linking. It could be argued that a world without such standards would quickly develop into anarchy, and discovery and access for scholars would be very difficult.

E-books

Colin Steele in his coverage of e-books in Chapter 4 states that: 'The challenge for 21st-century scholarship, which includes e-books, is to implement an infrastructure for the digital world untrammelled by the historical legacies in the frameworks and costings of print culture.' However, it is clear that we have not yet reached that Utopia.

Whereas journals have traditionally supported research activity within academic institutions, books have traditionally supported learning and teaching. Course textbooks, reading-list materials, scholarly monographs and reference materials have all been important library acquisitions for the student body.

The e-book market has been much slower in maturing than the e-journals market. In his book *Print is Dead*, Jeff Gomez (2008) traces the history of the comparatively slow introduction of the e-book. Librarians and users have been challenged by the plethora of e-book readers, the difficulty of reading books on screen, lack of interoperability between publisher and aggregator platforms, and the business models associated with e-book provision.

Librarians are keen to expand their e-book collections. In 2006 the Higher Education Consultancy Group undertook a survey of UK university libraries on behalf of the JISC E-Books Working Group (HECG, 2006); 89 out the 92 university libraries which responded said they were either 'eager' or 'very eager' to develop e-book collections. In addition, librarians told the consultants that they wanted: multiple and concurrent access for users (not one copy, one user); an easier way of discovering what e-books are available; and easy access for their users (not lots of different platforms and interfaces).

It is extremely difficult to obtain accurate and up-to-date statistics on e-books. However, in August 2009, Michael Smith, Head of the International Digital Publishing Forum, reported that e-book sales were up 149% on year to date. He went on to say: 'For me the most interesting thing is that these figures are likely soft, and the true market performance of e-books is probably stronger given that this data is for the US only' (Eltham, 2009).

One exciting new development which may very well impact on the availability of books for library users is the Espresso Book Machine (EBM). This is a print-on-demand machine that takes a PDF file and prints, collates, covers and binds it as a single paperback book in a matter of minutes. The machine is designed for the library and bookstore marketplace, and the first one was installed in the New York Public Library in 2007. The first one in the UK was launched in 2009 at Blackwell bookstore in Oxford: 'signalling the end, says Blackwell, to the frustration of being told by a bookseller that a title is out of print, or not in stock, the Espresso offers access to almost half a million books' (Flood, 2009) (and this will increase to over a million by the end of 2009).

Clearly, publishers see the growing demand from libraries for e-books and, as can seen from the above statistics, many are now providing both their current titles and back catalogues in e-format. They are also responding to the student and consumer demand for e-books to be read on mobile devices such as the Sony e-book reader, Amazon's Kindle and now the iPhone.

However, there is one category of e-book which publishers still remain reluctant to make available: that is the e-textbook.

In the UK, the JISC E-Books Working Group – which oversees e-book consortia activity – has been in repeated dialogue with publishers to persuade them to make their e-textbooks available to libraries – but to little avail. Publishers' overriding concern is that if they allow libraries to make e-textbooks available, the student market for textbooks will decline significantly. So, in 2007 funding was obtained to undertake an ambitious project, the National E-Book Observatory Project (JISC, 2007) – which would make high-demand reading-list texts free at the point of use to all students in the UK for a period of two years and monitor the use of those titles and the impact on publishers' sales. The key findings from the project were highly insightful. Students used the e-textbooks in huge numbers at all times of the day and night, rarely reading linearly, but skimming and dipping into the content; most reading was done on screen. However, the most significant findings were that the availability of the e-textbook did not impact upon the circulation of printed textbooks in library collections, and online availability had little impact upon publishers' sales. It is to be hoped that, following this project, publishers will be keener to sell e-textbooks to libraries.

The public library of the future

In a recent *Top Trends* blog on the future of public libraries, a long list of key influences on public libraries was posted. This included: sustainability; pricing (free versus user pays); trustworthiness of information; the value that the local community puts on information/knowledge; the pace of technological change; and democratization of information (Web 2.0, etc) (Macmanus, 2009). It is unlikely that anyone would disagree with this list. Public libraries always seem to be in the news with negative articles on library closures, reduced budgets, fewer staff and reduced spend on books. The pressure on public libraries is a worldwide phenomenon. A librarian in the USA contributed to the blog, writing: 'Unfortunately, the economic situation, e.g. sustainability (in California, at least) is starting to really rise to the top. In the short term, libraries will need to do more with less money, fewer staff, reduced hours, while at the same time demand is at an all time high' (Garza, 2009).

In the UK there have certainly been public library closures. Figures from the Chartered Institute of Public Finance and Accountancy (CIPFA) show that in 2005–6 there were 56 fewer central and branch libraries and 58 fewer mobile libraries than in 2001–2. But such bald figures hide the fact that urban and rural demographics change over the years and many libraries have extended their opening hours to accommodate evening and weekend activities and services. Moreover, CIPFA figures for 2007 show that there were over 337 million visits to over 4,700 public libraries, 315 million book issues, 64 million visits to library websites and a budget of over £1 billion (Harrison, 2008). However, it might be argued that public libraries do have an image problem. In the UK the House of Commons Culture, Media and Sports Select Committee agreed that 'a significant barrier to library use was shabby buildings, whether inside or out' (House of Commons Culture, Media and Sports Select Committee, 2005). There is no doubt that attractive buildings that are pleasant to visit and work in can enhance the position of the library in the local community. Childs (2006) points out that imaginative design in a number of recent new-build libraries (e.g. Peckham, Bournemouth, Cambridge) has caught the public's imagination.

When there is a debate about their future it seems to focus on either the traditionalist view of the 'book lobby', who maintain that libraries should be all about books and not much else, and the 'diversifiers', who believe that libraries should be more than just about books and should broaden their offering to encompass computing, multi-media, social space and learning programmes (Holden and Ezra, 2009). The reality of the situation is that public libraries should respond to the needs of the local area and the local community. In a deprived urban area, after-school homework clubs, internet access and literacy/language programmes might be appropriate, whereas in a remote rural area the service might wish to attract volunteers to help extend opening hours and provide a much-needed social and meeting space for local people. At a more strategic level, the (UK) Commission on Integration and Cohesion (2007) identified libraries as key partners in helping to promote integration, helping to dispel ignorance and prejudice about other cultures. There are many successful examples of such work, such as Manchester's initiative with the Pakistani community or Leicester's work with refugees as library volunteers – services tailored to reflect the local situation. A recent report from the British trade union Unison concludes that library service providers should work with their communities to shape services together:

> Libraries rest on a bed of goodwill from local communities. They are valued and trusted. But much more could and should be done to involve both the staff and the local communities in the shaping of the service. This should involve current users, the 'Friends of the Library' and support groups, but should also develop means of reaching out to those who currently do not use the library as well. (Davies, 2008)

There is clearly no 'one size fits all' model for public libraries of the future. Many, worldwide, are developing exciting and innovative 21st-century services for their communities. Some are becoming more like Starbucks – providing coffee shop services alongside internet access and traditional books and reference services. Others are working with minority groups or with teenagers in their area and providing support and even sometimes work experience for them. Book clubs, homework clubs, premises for local interest groups all abound. An article by Wooden (2006) examined the four areas of public library activity that resonated most with both the public and funders alike. These were: providing safe and productive activities and services for teenagers; helping address illiteracy and poor reading skills among adults; affording ready access to information about government services; and ensuring even greater access to computers for all. Perhaps a little unusual, but certainly a way to raise interest in public libraries, is a wonderful idea from Scandinavia which has recently been introduced to some UK public libraries – borrowing a person! To quote *The Times*:

> Instead of books, readers can come to the library and borrow a person for a 30-minute chat. The human 'books' on offer vary from event to event but always include a healthy cross-section of stereotypes. Last weekend, the small but richly diverse list included Police Officer, Vegan, Male Nanny and Lifelong Activist as well as Person with Mental Health Difficulties and Young Person Excluded from School.   (Baker, 2008)

Because public libraries do have a special place in the hearts of the general public it is likely that, in one manifestation or another, the concept will survive. But in the words of British Member of Parliament Lyn Brown in 2008:

> It seems to be that the original core purpose of libraries for information, education and culture still holds firm. But the world around continues to change at an ever increasing pace and libraries must embrace that social change and constantly adjust the manner, methodology and public face of how it continues to deliver this core purpose.
>
> (National Literacy Trust, 2008)

National libraries of the future

National libraries are generally funded by governments, firstly to act as repositories for the books, journals, heritage materials and grey literature published in a country, and secondly as centres to support research. This section focuses on new challenges faced by the British

Library, as a case study. However, these challenges are common to all national libraries around the world. How do they continue to collect and preserve information and knowledge that is no longer produced on paper, but in digital format? And how do they continue to meet the expectation that scholars and the general public will have access to that information and knowledge in perpetuity?

The British Library is one of the world's most significant research libraries, with a collection of more than 150 million items, including 14 million books, 920,000 journal and newspaper titles, 58 million patents and 3 million sound recordings.[4] Its historical treasures are numerous and include the Lindisfarne Gospels, the Magna Carta and many other important historical texts, maps and documents. The British Library is also a magnificent example of how a research library can meet the needs of many other diverse user groups, becoming not only a place for the serious scholar, but a cultural history centre and a support centre for small businesses. A visit to the building is a wonderful experience: inspiring architecture and good frappuccino either from a café in the courtyard, or, in poor weather, from an inside café. The British Library runs a programme of fascinating exhibitions which make its special collections accessible to the general public. At the time of writing, the British Library is providing an exhibition called 'Henry VIII: Man and Monarch', providing access to key documents from the life and times of the bloodthirsty king whose reign changed the nature of England. The British Library also offers stimulating workshops, activities and resources for teachers and learners of all ages. It supports entrepreneurs through its Business and IP [intellectual property] Centre, which provides not just published material but also courses, podcasts, webcasts and other events and services to support small and medium-sized businesses in the UK. Its website provides access to a range of digitized material and receives 67 million hits each year.

The British Library clearly operates at many levels. 'At the core it represents the collective memory of the nation by retaining for posterity the intellectual output of British publishing' (British Library, n.d.). Legal deposit is the legislation that requires publishers and distributors in the UK and the Republic of Ireland to send one copy of each of their publications to the Legal Deposit Office of the British Library within one month of publication. The British Library adds to this core collection by purchasing research-level material from around the world.

The purpose of this is to be the library of 'first instance and last resort; last resort for those whose primary access is their university, company or public library and first instance where the Library is the sole convenient source for the research material they require'.[5]

The Library, then, has to care for its collections, and 190 professional staff are dedicated to preserving the print collections. It has also to provide access to the collections in its readings rooms, which are in the beautiful new building at St Pancras, London. The building was completed in 1997 by Colin St John Wilson, with generous public spaces and seats for 1480 readers. Despite the Library being housed in a state-of-the-art building, capacity in the reading rooms has been an issue of controversy. The author Christopher Hawtree reported that he had to 'perch on a windowsill'. The historian Lady Antonia Fraser complained: 'I had to queue for 20 minutes to get in, in freezing weather. Then I queued to leave my coat for 20 minutes [at the compulsory check-in]. Then half an hour to get my books and another 15 minutes to get my coat. I'm told it's due to students having access now. Why can't they go to their university libraries? It's become a social gathering.' (Alberge, 2008).

These comments illustrate one of the problems facing the British Library in the modern world. It is required to satisfy differing expectations and to provide access to a wide diversity of users. Students and researchers all need and expect access to scholarly materials. In the physical world a 15-minute wait is cause for complaint and in the digital world research indicates that users also show 'impatience in search and navigation, and zero tolerance for any delay in satisfying their information needs' (CIBER, 2008).

In her introduction to *The British Library Strategy 2008–2011*, the Chief Executive, Dame Lynne Brindley, sums up the challenge of providing researchers and students with the critical mass of digital content they demand:

> The environment in which we operate has arguably changed more in the past two decades than in the preceding two centuries, driven particularly by technological developments. Such change is gradually transforming traditional scholarly dependency on the physical library as a major source for meeting research needs into a complex network of options, with varying levels of accessibility, authoritativeness and depth.
> (British Library, 2007)

The British Library must therefore not only continue to increase its collection of print material through legal deposit, but also extend its collection building to digital content. The idea of legal deposit dates back several hundred years and is well suited to print publications, but it does not work well in the e-environment. With an increasing volume of important material published in e-format, primary legislation for extending legal deposit to electronic publications has been in place since 2003, but progress towards the secondary legislation has been slow. There are a number of reasons for this. First, there is the issue of the place of publication. In the print world it is fairly easy to identify the place where an item was published, but when material is published on the internet, traditional boundaries are removed. An item published in one country can be easily accessed elsewhere, and other countries may want to archive it and their users may want to access it.

The second issue is the funding, the development and, more crucially, the sustainability of the robust technical architecture required to archive and preserve huge amounts of digital information. The technological issues lie not only with the infrastructure but also with the processes that will allow the content to be read by future generations. Technology transfers in recent history have illustrated the problem. For example, information stored just a few years ago on floppy discs might well by now have become corrupted, even if a machine could still be located to provide access to the stored information. The issue of technical obsolescence has to be addressed if the British Library is not to amass a collection of bytes than cannot be read.

Perhaps the most challenging issue is how the British Library provides access to this vast array of born-digital content. The role which national libraries undertake in preserving material for the long term does not equate to making that material available over the internet. The British Library does indeed provide open access to its catalogue and it has also digitized and made available online much of the material in its out-of-copyright collections. Moreover, it has digitized and made available other collections where copyright still applies, notably many thousands of pages of newspaper archives and many hours of audio recordings. Although these digitized collections are available on the internet, they are only accessible via an authentication system. This means that only UK higher and further education institutions that sign a licence with the British Library have access. These collections are not available to the general public or to the lone scholar.

The crux of the problem is how to provide remote online access to material still in copyright while protecting the interests of the rights holders. Recently, Dame Lynne Brindley pointed out:

> We are in danger of an escalating arms race between geeks/hackers and tech savvy young people and businesses focussed on lock-down – the music industry has shown the difficulties of DRM [digital rights management] based strategies. Let's put equal imagination into workable new business models! And we should be aware of trends towards more open innovation models – in software standards, in publishing, in education courseware and in source code. The required innovation balance is not a straightforward one.
>
> (British Library, 2009)

Finding the balance is not easy because the users and creators of information have completely different expectations. Researchers and students increasingly expect that the British Library's collection of the 'world's knowledge' will be available not only by visiting the reading rooms, but also remotely to their desktops. Authors and publishers expect to earn money through the digital distribution of their content. Will the balance be found and will the British Library (and other national libraries) be able to embrace new technologies and connect users in innovative ways with the content they need? Or will use of the library's collections, whether paper or digital, require the time and resources necessary to visit the reading rooms at St Pancras?

The librarian of the future

If this is the way academic, public and national libraries are evolving, what does that mean for the role of librarians? While in many libraries footfall is declining, the use of the digital library is soaring. Students, researchers and the general public no longer need to come to the physical library to consult printed documents, but they do still come to find quiet study space, to work on group projects, to seek the advice of information professionals or just to meet friends socially for coffee. Most libraries now, while continuing to provide facilities for face-to-face interactions with users, also provide services for remote users. This may be via an 'ask a librarian' chat line, e-mail, telephone or online tutorials. With dwindling shelf space devoted to printed items, and with remote assistance and support for users, we can but wonder about the future of the physical library – but what of the staff? It seems clear that as long as universities, colleges and schools exist as physical entities there will continue to be a requirement for information to inform and support learning, teaching and research. And the general public appears to have a growing appetite for information, from freely available sources on the internet to quality-assured information from reputable publishers.

At the beginning of this chapter we discussed the importance of both the surface web and the deep web. Unless all information becomes 'toll free' (and that seems unlikely in the short to medium term) then there will continue to be a need for e-resource acquisition, organization and management, as well as information literacy training – and these require staff. Furthermore, evidence from the library satisfaction survey LibQUAL+ shows that staff and students value support and assistance from information professionals very highly (Stanley and Killick, 2009). So, while the role and skills set of the librarian will alter radically and many of the traditional activities of librarians will disappear, there will almost certainly be a requirement for staff in the digital information universe. However, librarians should heed the words of Chris Batt, CEO of the Museums, Libraries and Archives Council, speaking as long ago as 2000. He said that librarians needed to step up to the mark in the digital age and that 'there needs to be a fundamental shift in how librarians are trained and how they perceive their roles' (Batt, 2000). Information professionals need to be committed to changing the relationship between information and the people who want it. We will need new skills, new organizational structures and new partnerships. Change is already under way but clearly more work remains to be done.

The bookshop of the future

The novelist Susan Hill recently wrote, 'Whenever I hear people shouting, "Save the village store", I wonder if they have been in one lately, and the same goes for bookshops' (Hill, 2006). Times are tough for bookshops, in particular for independent bookshops. The business is often inefficiently run, with understocking, overstocking and limited shelf space. It is difficult for them to compete with the large chains, supermarkets and in particular with Amazon, as each tries to undercut the others. The most recent Harry Potter novel has a published list price of £16.99, but Amazon is selling it for £4.99 and it was reported that one supermarket was selling it for £2.99. It would seem that Amazon is the 'big gorilla' in the booksellers' market. It can sell more books more cheaply, it does not have a shelf-space problem, it can site its warehouses in low-cost areas, and does not need to rent expensive retail outlets on the high street.

Changes in technology which provide the ability to sell cheaply have impacted on the bookselling business before. Charles Edward Maudie founded his circulating library in London in the 1840s and in the following 20 years it expanded to become a dominant force in the UK book trade. Like Amazon today, Maudie took advantage of the new technologies of the time: rail, steamship and the postal services. Like Amazon, Maudie was also able to sell cheaply. For the annual fee of one guinea, the customer was entitled to the loan of a volume which could be exchanged as often as one wished, and this was at a time when the average three-volume novel cost a guinea-and-a-half (£1.57). Maudie enjoyed a near monopoly and could claim huge discounts of around 50% from the publishers. This monopoly was finally challenged with the abolition of the three-decker novel in favour of the single-volume, six-shilling (30p) novel.

An interesting thing about Maudie's model is that the purchaser leased rather than bought the book. This model is one already in operation in the DVD market. For example, LOVEFiLM allows subscribers to choose from a library of over 65,000 films. The DVD is delivered by post the next day, and can be kept for an undefined period of time, with no late-return fees. Once the users have finished with films, they return them and another film of their choice is sent the next day. Membership fees are low, around £3 to £15 per month and the number of loans is unlimited. A similar model might work with e-books, providing that the right technology, digital rights management and e-book reader were available.

Is it possible that the Kindle and other portable e-book readers are going to provide alternative models of access and purchase and, in the process, make booksellers obsolete? These devices are already lighter and thinner than the typical paperback and provide mobile access to books, newspapers and journals. By using the keyboard of some of the more sophisticated e-book readers, users can add annotations to text, just as they might write in the margins of a book. And because it is digital, they can edit, delete and export their notes, highlight key passages and bookmark pages for future use.

Arguably, there will still be a market for illustrated books, the books we want as artefacts, but perhaps the paperback novel will go the way of vinyl record. Enthusiasts will use printed books, but the general public will prefer the convenience and portability of the e-book. They will be able to download titles from Amazon and other internet booksellers, just as they now download music to their iPods. Consumers will no longer have to think about how many books they can conveniently fit in their briefcases or suitcases; they will be able to carry a small library on a handy portable device when travelling.

Stephen Moss interviewed a number of independent booksellers for a report published in the *Guardian* newspaper in 2006 (Moss, 2006). Almost all of the booksellers interviewed recognized that if they were to have a sustainable future they could not just rely on selling books. One interviewee said: 'We're not just a bookshop. We're an information centre and a hub of activity.' An urban bookseller said: 'The moment I saw this shop and the market, I knew it was better than Brick Lane [in London] for a bookshop because it's a community street', and a rural bookseller said: 'People also realise the social importance of having a bookshop in a small town. It does more than sell books.' Wherever they are situated, these booksellers see that their future lies in becoming a part of the community, and offering services as well as selling books. Services may include the obvious, such as a coffee shop and book readings, but bookshops may also become centres for specialist information and training. They may also become providers of print on demand facilities. *Time* magazine called the Espresso Book Machine (described earlier in this chapter) the 'Invention of the Year' (Flood, 2009). Publishers and booksellers alike see the huge potential of a machine that collapses the supply chain, increases backlist sales, and matches supply with demand.

The publishing industry of the future

The publishing industry has developed its business models around printed books and journals as the major vehicle for the distribution of information. Timo Hannay of Nature Publishing has written: 'The web is the most disruptive influence on publishing since the invention of movable type . . . And now we have at our disposal the most powerful information dissemination tool in publishing history' (Hannay, 2007). Ian Russell in Chapter 3 also alludes to the disruptive influences on publishing in periods of rapid change. The internet has indeed turned publishing on its head, and publishers of all types are torn between the desire to protect the established models and the desire to experiment with the brave new world of the internet. The creative industries are essential to the UK's future competitiveness and it is estimated that by 2020 they will generate over 11% of gross value added (GVA), which is the difference between output and intermediate consumption for any given sector, used in the estimation of gross domestic product (GDP), and is a key indicator of the state of the whole economy. How is this business to be stimulated and expanded in a world which expects information to be delivered over the internet, and often for free?

Journal publishers were the first to make a transition to e-publishing, and most academic journals are now published in electronic form. Journal publishers were the first to migrate to the internet for two reasons, the first being that their predominant business model is sales to institutions and not to individuals. Institutional libraries pay for print subscriptions and make those journals available to their patrons. Thus the print model is easily transferred to the electronic world. The second reason why the journal has migrated so quickly to the internet is that it is simply a 'wrapper' for collections of self-contained articles. Online access and technology are capable of providing fast searching and direct access to the article.

There are three unique aspects to the journal publishing business. First, the publisher does not pay the authors for their content. Academic authors write for recognition, not money. Second, journal publishing operates in a market which is not normal. Each journal is unique and no one journal can substitute for another. Thus, journal publishers may compete for authors and for market share, but they do not experience the direct competition that generally happens in other markets. Third, customers generally pay in advance, usually annually, before the product is created or distributed.

Journal publishers, especially the large ones, who are able to provide a critical mass of quality content supported by cutting-edge technology, are in a very strong position. However, despite these strengths, the journal publishing industry does face threats. There is a groundswell of opinion that the outputs of scholarly research, funded by public money, should be unrestricted and open to all users on the internet without financial or other barriers. This is known as Open Access (OA), as discussed earlier in this chapter and by other contributors to this book.

The debate between the pro-OA lobby and the scholarly publishing industry has been fierce, with the publishers defending their business model and pointing out the value they bring to the process in terms of organizing peer review, editorial review and, of course, the organization of articles into discipline-specific journals. On the other hand, there are those who argue that, in the age of the internet, the role of the scholarly publisher is no longer required. Indeed it is true that all the functions of the publisher could quite easily be undertaken by the author and his or her peers. In the age of the desktop, typesetting is not required, social networking could facilitate a new form of peer review and articles could be distributed from authors' websites.

Taken to its conclusion, such a model for the publication of scholarly material might very well create anarchy. Journal publishers would go out of business and researchers would not have the motivation to publish. They would not receive the registration and recognition provided by the current publishing system. If they did continue to publish, there would be hundreds of thousands of journal articles each year, distributed across thousands of websites. Users would have great difficulty in finding articles or understanding their provenance.

OA proponents have suggested that there is still a role for publishers in this model – the role of providing 'overlay services'. In this model, the journal publisher is no longer the distributor of content but becomes the provider of specialist peer-review services such as interfaces to articles deposited in institutional or subject repositories, guaranteeing that they have passed the journal's quality standards. This model offers small comfort for the shareholders of the large publishing houses. The change from being the distributor of unique content to that of being one of many firms competing to provide editorial services is not compelling. No wonder that the journal publishing industry is so keen to refute the potential benefits of 'green' OA. Nonetheless, it would seem that the future will provide increasing amounts of literature openly available. Copyright has been a barrier in the past, but now around 80–90% of publication channels allow authors to deposit papers on their own websites or in a repository after an embargo period following publication in a journal. Some journal publishers have gone further; *Nature*, for example, does not demand copyright from its authors but merely a licence to publish, leaving copyright with the authors or their institutions. Publishers also recognize that universities want to showcase their research outputs, and some are already offering universities metadata, so that institutional repositories can point to articles that are on the publishers' websites. This has the advantage, from the publishers' point of view, of allowing institutional repositories bibliographic information and metadata, while firmly keeping control of the PDF versions of articles.

However, a more ordered future might see publishers and academia using technology to widen access to scholarly material and innovating scholarly discourse.

For example, some publishers have been fast to seize the opportunities provided by social networking and Web 2.0 technologies and have moved into that space themselves. Nature Publishing Group launched one of the first scientific social networking sites with Nature Network in 2007. This site allows scientists to build networks of contacts and talk about research and scientific issues; its functionality includes blogs and interactive forums for the exchange of ideas. The Royal Society of Chemistry has recently acquired ChemSpider, an OA online database of structure-searchable chemical information, which allows researchers to collaborate and share data. Nature Network and ChemSpider are free to use, and allow their publishers to engage in a radically new way with customers and communities of scientists. In a world of globalization, Web 2.0 technologies perhaps provide scholars with a means of personal contact that they have not had since the early learned societies of the 17th century, when communication between scholars depended on the attendance of meetings rather than communication through publication (Wells, 1999).

The debate about OA looks set to roll on for many years and this is not surprising, given the business at stake. As Steven Pearlstein has written:

> There is nothing more amusing than watching business interests work
> themselves up into righteous frenzy over a threat to their monopoly
> profits from a new technology or some upstart with a different business
> model; the monopolists (or their first cousins the oligopolists) try to
> present themselves as the champions of the consumer, or defenders of a
> level playing field, as if they had not become ridiculously rich by
> sticking it to consumers and enjoying years in which the playing field
> was tilted to their advantage. (Pearlstein, 2006)

Journal publishing is not the only area of the publishing industry that will
change. Publishers of reference material have been close on the heels of
the journal publishers in the move to the internet. Reference publishing
business has transferred well to the internet, because of its business
model, largely sales to libraries rather than to the individual, and because
its format works more effectively when published as a database. Database
organization and web functionality mean that reference entries can be much
more easily searched than is possible in the print world. An example is
the *Oxford Dictionary of National Biography*. In the print format it is 60
volumes of 56,862 entries. Entries are organized in the usual alphabetical
order, and the user needs to know what they are looking for in order to
find it. With web technology the online version of the *Oxford Dictionary
of National Biography* is always fully up to date, and it can be searched in
seconds. Searches can be organized by the name of an individual, but also
by place, a particular sphere of activity, or within a particular time. Such
a search might take years using the 60 volumes of the printed book.

However, despite the wonderful functionality of the reference
database, the future of the reference publisher is not certain. There is a
significant threat in the form of Wikipedia. Will publishers of
subscription material on the invisible web be able to compete with the
visible and free Wikipedia?

While journal and reference publishers have made the transition to
online publishing, other sectors of the publishing industry have been
slow to make the move or have actively resisted it. One of the main
drivers of resistance is the lessons learned from the music publishing
industry and the fear that electronic books will be illegally downloaded,
shared and pirated (Pearlstein, 2006).

Most resistant to a move to electronic platforms are the textbook
publishers. The bulk of their revenues come not from libraries but from

individuals. Libraries want to buy e-textbooks, but this demand has been resisted because 'free at the point of use' access via the library might destroy the traditional model, which is sale to the individual student. There has also been, until now, little demand from the public for e-books, but it would seem that the emergence of e-book readers such as the Kindle and the Sony e-book reader or the next generation of such devices may well provide the publishing industry with its 'iPod moment'. The iPod is ubiquitous and music is generally acquired by download. This has meant a huge change for the music industry and a radical change in the business models it uses. Currently, where Amazon has books available in both print and e-book format, the electronic versions have sales of 35% of the same books in print (Schonlfeld, 2009). Andrew Marr has written: 'But it's clear enough that after all the waiting and the over-hyping, the e-book is arriving. Before long you are going to see them being carried nonchalantly around' (Marr, 2007).

Some publishers have seen other benefits of the move to the electronic medium. Victoria Barnsley, the CEO of Harper Collins, pointed out that the e-book offers publishers an end to unwanted inventory, no more returns, no more out of print titles and greater value attached to obscure titles (Barnsley, 2008). She sees not only the advantages of electronic publication in terms of publishing administration, but also the possibilities of Web 2.0 technologies for a new type of publishing, which she describes as the 'circular model', with authors and readers interacting with each other as part of the publishing process. An example of this is the online publication of Doris Lessing's *The Golden Notebook* project. Seven readers kept public journals on their thoughts while reading the book, and other readers commented, generating an ongoing discussion in the novel's on-screen margins. As fascinating as this project is, the business model that would sustain such publishing is as yet uncertain. Barnsley said it would be difficult to establish a profitable pricing model when most consumers were used to free digital content, but nonetheless predicted that 'within say 10 years more than half our sales will come from digital downloads'. She has been quoted as saying that the Kindle, with its wireless connection, will enable impulse shopping: 'Imagine watching Cranford on the TV, and immediately downloading the complete works of Elizabeth Gaskell – instant bedtime reading' (Barnsley, 2008).

Another book publisher ready to experiment is Bloomsbury

Academic, which has announced a new 'Science Ethics and Innovation' series edited by Sir John Huston. The series will be available free for non-commercial use over the internet under a Creative Commons Licence, with the publisher estimating that the cost of publication can be recouped thorough sales of hard copies that will be printed via print-on-demand and short-run printing technologies. The publisher Frances Pinter estimates that Bloomsbury will have to sell around 200 copies of a highly technical monograph, priced at around £50, to make a profit, and believes it will take two years to judge whether the model is financially viable. Pinter has pointed out that if publishers do not experiment with such models, academics will bypass publishers (Page, 2009).

It would seem that whatever the area of publishing examined, journals, reference materials, books or newspapers, the internet is disrupting long-established business models and means of distribution. Take, for example, another relatively new start-up enterprise – Mendeley. Founded by three German academics and now based in London, Mendeley allows authors to 'drag and drop' research papers into its site, which automatically extracts keywords, cited references, etc., and creates a searchable database. Mendeley say that instead of authors waiting to be published and for citations to appear, they could move to a regime of 'real time' citations, thereby greatly reducing the time taken for research to be applied in the real world. The site already contains over 4 million scientific papers and 60,000 people have already signed up (Mendeley Research Networks, undated).

Some publishers' response will be to invest in preserving the status quo rather than in adapting to the changing world. For others there are undoubted opportunities to monetize new web technologies and formats such as the e-book. However, as discussed earlier in this chapter, the biggest threat to traditional publishing comes in the form of Google. Not only is it digitizing books in their millions, it is also challenging the publishing industry in other areas. Google Scholar, which searches peer-reviewed abstracts and articles from academic publishers, is challenging the established publishers of abstracting and indexing databases. Those established databases are sold on subscription to libraries, and users need to authenticate in order to use them. How much easier it is to use the freely and easily available Google Scholar – often good enough and in time. Google Maps not only challenges the traditional map publishers and vendors of geospatial data, but also creates dependencies on Google because it powers many map-based services, embedded on third-party websites. What happens when a company creates these dependencies and then takes the content away, or decides to charge for it?

Google has also recently launched Knol, a website which at first glance is a challenge to Wikipedia, but is trying to go a little further. The articles on Knol can have multiple (but named) authors, which, under Google's structure, is called 'moderated collaboration'.

Final thoughts

Perhaps all stakeholders in the current traditional information landscape have some lessons to learn from Google. On its corporate information web page Google lists ten things it has found to be true. The first of these is 'Focus on the user and all else will follow', and to this end Google ensures that:

- the interface is clear and simple
- pages load instantly
- placement in search results is never sold to anyone
- advertising on the site must offer relevant content and not be a distraction.

Will traditional publishers and librarians focus on the user and find that 'all else follows' or will many fail to find new methods of access, dissemination, distribution and business models to support them? The danger is that they do not, and that Google becomes a monopoly. Do we want one single organization controlling the whole information environment? Google claims that 'You can make money without doing evil', but a monopoly is a dangerous thing. If librarians and publishers do not adapt, evolve and survive, there is the danger that Google could not only become the ultimate organizer of the world's information, but also the ultimate controller of information, the censor and the spy.

Cory Doctorow commenting on Google recently wrote: 'There's no dictator benevolent enough to entrust with the power to determine our political, commercial, social and ideological agenda' (Doctorow, 2009).

That would seem obvious, but what is not so obvious is the

organization of a public intervention that would provide governance, regulation and ensure *order*.

Notes

1   http://arxiv.org.
2   www.pubmedcentral.nih.gov.
3   www.rluk.ac.uk/node/85.
4   www.bl.uk/aboutus/quickinfo/facts/index.html [accessed 28 September 2009].
5   www.bl.uk/aboutus/stratpolprog/coldevpol/index.html [accessed 28 September 2009].

References

Alberge, D. (2008) Frustration for Authors as Students Hog British Library Reading Rooms, *The Times*, 21 April 2008.

ARL (Association of Research Libraries) (2009) *The University's Role in the Dissemination of Research and Scholarship: a call to action*, Association of Research Libraries,
www.arl.org/bm~doc/disseminating-research-feb09.pdf [accessed 22 September 2009].

Baker, D. (2008) The New Library Fad: borrow a person, *The Times*, 22 April,
http://women.timeslonline.co.uk/tol/life_and_style/women/the_way_we_live/article3790377.ece [accessed 28 September 2009].

Barnsley, V. (2008) *Publishing: media's last diehard?*, talk given at the London School of Economics, 4 November, reported in *The Bookseller*, 5 November 2008, and on the Times Emit blog available at
http://aptstudio.com/timesemit/2008/11/05/victoria-barnsley-harpercollins-ceo-on-publishing-medias-last-diehard/ [accessed 28 September 2009].

Batt, C. (2000) Public Libraries in a Wired World, paper given at ALIA 2000, *Capitalising on Knowledge: the information profession in the 21st century*, Canberra, 24–26 October, Canberra: Australian Library and Information Association, 2000,
http://conferences.alia.org.au/alia2000/proceedings/chris.batt.html [accessed 28 September 2009].

Binfield, P. (2009) PLoS One: background, future development, and article-level metrics. In Mornati, S. and Hedlund, T. (eds), *Rethinking Electronic Publishing: innovations in communication paradigms and technologies*, Proceedings of the 13th International Conference on Electronic Publishing, Milan, Italy, 10–12 June, 69–86,

http://conferences.aepic.it/index.php/elpub/elpub2009/paper/view/114/51
[accessed 25 September 2009].

British Library (n.d.) *Collections Development Policy*,
www.bl.uk/aboutus/stratpolprog/coldevpol/index.html.

British Library (2007) *The British Library's Strategy 2008-2011*, 2007. Available at
www.bl.uk/aboutus/stratpolprog/strategy0811/strategy2008-2011.pdf.

British Library (2009) *Intellectual Property: the British Library's perspective*,
www.bl.uk/ip/ [accessed 28 September 2009].

Childs, P. (2006) Sssh! The quiet revolution, *New Library World*, 107 (3/4), 149–56,
www.ingentaconnect.com/content/mcb/072/2006/00000107/F0020003/
art00006 [accessed 25 September 2009].

CIBER (Centre for Information Behaviour and the Evaluation of Research) (2008)
Information Behaviour of the Researcher of the Future, a CIBER briefing paper,
University College London,
www.ucl.ac.uk/infostudies/research/ciber/downloads/ggexecutive.pdf [accessed
29 September 2009].

Commission on Integration and Cohesion (2007) *Our Shared Future*, final report of
the Commission on Integration and Cohesion,
http://collections.europarchive.org/tna/20080726153624/www.
integrationandcohesion.org.uk/~/media/assets/www.integrationandcohesion.
org.uk/our_shared_future%20pdf.ashx [accessed 25 September 2009].

Davies, S. (2008) *Taking Stock: the future of our public library service*, an independent
report for Unison, September, www.unison.org.uk/acrobat/17301.pdf [accessed
25 September 2009].

Doctorow, C. (2009) Search Is Too Important to Leave to One Company – even
Google, *Guardian*, 2 June,
www.guardian.co.uk/technology/2009/jun/01/search-public-google-privacy-
rights [accessed 28 September 2009].

Duddy, C. (2009) A Personal Perspective on Accessing Academic Information in the
Google Era, or, How I learned to stop worrying and love Google, *Serials*, 22
(2), 131–5,
http://uksg.metapress.com/media/b0cyhcturk6yphxqmxfr/contributions/
u/7/6/2/u762p55437658x7w.pdf [accessed 22 September 2009].

EDL (European Digital Library) Foundation (2007) *European Digital Library
Homepage*, http://dev.europeana.eu/edlnet/edl_foundation/purpose.php [accessed
22 September 2009].

Edwards, R. (2006) The Learning Grid at the University of Warwick: a library
innovation to support learning in higher education, *Sconul Focus*, 38, 4–7,

www.sconul.ac.uk/publications/newsletter/38/2.pdf [accessed 25 September 2009].

Eltham, K. (2009) E-book Sales Up 149% YTD, Reports IDPF, *Electric Alphabet*, 13 August,
www.electricalphabet.net/2009/08/13/ebook-sales-up-149-ytd-reports-idpf/ [accessed 28 September 2009].

Flood, A. (2009) Revolutionary Espresso Book Machine Launches in London, *The Guardian*, 24 April,
www.guardian.co.uk/books/2009/apr/24/espresso-book-machine-launches [accessed 28 September 2009].

Frean, A. (2008) White Bread for Young Minds, Says University of Brighton Professor, *The Times*, 14 January,
http://technology.timesonline.co.uk/tol/news/tech_and_web/the_web/article3182091.ece [accessed 22 September 2009].

Garza, R. (2009) In Response to R. Macmanus, The Future of Public Libraries, *What's Next: Top Trends*, June,
http://toptrends.nowandnext.com/?p=603 [accessed 25 September 2009].

Gomez, J. (2008) *Print is Dead: books in our digital age*, Macmillan,
http://books.google.co.uk/books?id=WYnQE-WFQxgC&printsec=frontcover&dq=gomez+print+is+dead&ei=Oo7ASuWEHI6OzATEiPWtDw#v=onepage&q=&f=false [accessed 28 September 2009].

Google (2009) *Google Books: library partners: Bavarian State Library*,
http://books.google.com/googlebooks/partners.html [accessed 22 September 2009].

Hannay, T. (2007) The Web Opportunity, *Nascent, Nature's* blog on web technology and science, 29 June,
http://blogs.nature.com/wp/nascent/2007/06/post.html [accessed 28 September 2009].

Harnad, S., Brody, T., Vallières, F., Carr, L., Hitchcock, S., Gingras, Y., Oppenheim, C., Stamerjohanns, H. and Hilf, E. R. (2004) The Access/Impact Problem and the Green and Gold Roads to Open Access, *Serials Review*, **30** (4), 310–14,
http://users.ecs.soton.ac.uk/harnad/Temp/impact.html [accessed 22 September 2009].

Harrison, J. (2008) *Public Libraries have Massive Support but are challenged to do Better as Annual Stats Explode Myths*, Birmingham: Museums, Libraries and Archives Council,
www.mla.gov.uk/news_and_views/press/releases/2008/Public-libraries-massive-support [accessed 28 September 2009].

HECG (Higher Education Consultancy Group) (2006) *A Feasibility Study on the Acquisition of Books by HE Libraries and the Role of JISC*, London: JISC Collections, www.jisc.ac.uk/media/documents/jisc_collections/ebooks%20final%20report%205%20oct.doc [accessed 25 September 2009].

Hill, S. (2006) How David can Fight Goliath, *Guardian*, 14 January, www.guardian.co.uk/books/2006/jan/14/featuresreviews.guardianreviews17 [accessed 3 November 1009].

Holden, J. and Ezra, Y. (2009) Fact and Fiction: the future of public libraries, *Hantsweb*, http://www3.hants.gov.uk/library/future-libraries.htm [accessed 3 November 2009].

House of Commons Culture, Media and Sport Select Committee (2005) *Public Libraries, Third Report of Session, 2004-05*, www.publications.parliament.uk/pa/cm200405/cmselect/cmcumeds/81/81i.pdf [accessed 3 November 2009].

JISC (2007) *JISC National E-books Observatory Project*, www.jiscebooksproject.org/ [accessed 25 September 2009].

JISC (2009) Libraries Unleashed: colleges, universities and the digital challenge, *Guardian supplement*, 22 April, http://education.guardian.co.uk/librariesunleashed [accessed 22 September 2009].

Library of Congress (2009) Library of Congress Leads Nationwide Digitization Effort, *News from the Library of Congress*, 14 January, www.loc.gov/today/pr/2009/09-10.html [accessed 22 September 2009].

Mabe, M. (2006) (Electronic) Journals Publishing. In *The E-Resources Management Handbook*, UK Serials Group, http://uksg.metapress.com/media/fl9xa5turk6wvj768x2m/contributions/3/c/v/j/3cvjfqplkkemj3w0.pdf [accessed 22 September 2009].

Macmanus, R. (2009) The Future of Public Libraries: what's next, *Top Trends*, June, http://toptrends.newandnext.com/?p=603 [accessed 22 September 2009].

Marr, A. (2007) Curling Up With a Good Ebook, *Guardian*, 11 May, www.guardian.co.uk/technology/2007/may/11/news.newmedia?gusrc=rssfeed=1 [accessed 25 September 2009].

Mendeley Research Networks (undated) *Organize, Share and Discover Research Papers*, www.mendeley.com/ [accessed 28 September 2009].

Moss, S. (2006) The Best Sellers, *Guardian*, 22 May, www.guardian.co.uk/books/2006/may/22/bestukbookshops [accessed 28 September 2009].

National Literacy Trust (2008) Speech by Lynn Brown MP at the joint conference of CILIP's Branch and Mobile Libraries Group and Public Libraries Group, Wyboston Lakes, 13 June, www.literacytrust.org.uk/policy/LynBrownSpeech.doc [accessed 25 September 2009].

Norris, M., Oppenheim, C. and Rowland, F. (2008) The Citation Advantage of Open Access Articles, *Journal of the American Society of Information Science and Technology*, 59 (12), http://www3.interscience.wiley.com/journal/120748494/abstract?CRETRY=1&SRETRY=0 [accessed 22 September 2009].

Page, B. (2009) Bloomsbury Unveils Academic Imprint, *The Bookseller*, 5 September, www.thebookseller.com/news/66448-bloomsbury-unveils-academic-imprint.html [accessed 28 September 2009].

Pearlstein, S. (2006) A Sound Marketplace for Recorded Music, *The Washington Post*, 19 July, D01, www.washingtonpost.com/wp-dyn/content/article/2006/07/18/AR2006071801538.html?nav=emailpage [accessed 28 September 2009].

RIN (Research Information Network) (2009) *E-journals: their use, value and impact*, www.rin.ac.uk/use-ejournals [accessed 22 September 2009].

Schonfeld, E. (2009) For Books Available on Kindle, Sales Are now Tracking at 35 Percent of Print Sales, *TechCrunch*, 6 May, www.techcrunch.com/2009/05/06/for-books-available-on-kindle-sales-are-now-tracking-at-35-percent-of-print-sales/ [accessed 28 September 2009].

Stanley, T., and Killick, S. A. (2009) *Library Performance Measurement in the UK and Ireland*, Association of Research Libraries.

Sykes, J. (2008) Large-scale Digitization: the £22 million JISC programme and the role of libraries, *Serials*, 21 (3), 167–73, http://uksg.metapress.com/media/pf9dmxgjtk0qwk4aequy/contributions/a/2/2/8/a228n817471242g9.pdf [accessed 22 September 2009].

Wells, A. (1999) Exploring the Development of the Independent, Electronic, Scholarly Journal, MSc dissertation, University of Sheffield, http://panizzi.shef.ac.uk/elecdiss/edl0001/index.html [accessed 28 September 2009].

Williams, P. (2009) Book Review: going beyond Google, *Information World Review*, 9 April, www.iwr.co.uk/information-world-review/features/2240219/dig-deep-research-victories [accessed 22 September 2009].

Wooden, R. (2006) The Future of Public Libraries in an Internet Age, *National Civic Review*, Winter, 3–7, www.ncl.org/publications/ncr/95-4/0107libraries.pdf [accessed 28 September 2009].

Woodward, H. and Rowland, F. (2009) E-journals and E-books. In Baker, D. and Evans, W. (eds), *Digital Library Economics: an academic perspective*, Chandos Publishing, 161–75.

2

Scholarly communications: the view from the library

Rick Anderson

Where we are now: two crises for libraries, one crisis for publishers

Our current situation is highly unsettled. Three primary factors combine to threaten both the ongoing viability of scholarly publishers and the traditional position of academic libraries as information brokers and intermediaries. The first two, the crisis of searching and finding, and the crisis of the collection, stem from radical changes in the information environment, fostered by the advent of digital technology in general in the 20th century, and the emergence of Google in particular. The third, the crisis of price, has been looming for decades (Panitch and Michalak, 2005), and has been discussed and debated at length for almost as long.

Libraries – the crisis of searching and finding

Google's stated reason for being is to 'organize the world's information'. However, its actual modus operandi is much more ingenious than that. In fact, what Google's search engine does is *interrogate* the world's information – not all of it, but a far larger portion of it than any single library could ever hope to own, let alone index. Having interrogated the information, Google then organizes the search results by relevance. The company is notoriously (if understandably) cagey about its exact methods of relevance ranking, saying only that relevance is assessed 'by considering over a hundred factors, including how many other pages link to the page, the positions of the search terms within the page, and the proximity of the search terms to one another' (Blachman and Peek, 2007). Google's use of external links to assess relevance is particularly noteworthy, and while it is far from a foolproof system, it is much more effective than traditional relevance ranking, which is usually based on the prevalence of search terms. To illustrate the difference: when processing a search for the terms 'westminster', 'abbey' and 'london', a search engine using traditional relevance ranking will identify as many websites as possible containing those terms, and will place at the top of the result set those websites that contain the most repetitions of those three words. Google will also gather as many websites as possible, but will place at the top of the result set those sites to which many other sites have linked. This ranking method does a far better job than prevalence ranking does of identifying sites that are considered by other websites to be authoritative. So, while a search for 'westminster', 'abbey' and 'london' on a traditional search engine will identify the site that talks most about those terms, Google will show you the site that is most broadly considered to be an authoritative one as regards those terms – and thereby almost guarantees that the top search result will be, in fact, the official website of Westminster Abbey in London.

The reason for explaining, however simplistically and partially, the logic behind Google's ranking strategies is to compare them with the organizational strategies used by libraries. Libraries traditionally take a completely different approach: whereas the researcher using Google begins by interrogating an astronomically huge number of documents, a subset of which is then organized by Google into an ingeniously prioritized search result, libraries gather selected documents first, then allow patrons to search the selection indirectly by means of proxy documents (catalogue records). In the traditional library, documents not owned by the library are not available for searching and the documents owned by the library are not searchable directly; only their proxies can be searched, and only by means of library-specified criteria such as author, title, standardized subject heading or (more recently) keyword.

Before the mass migration of information production into the digital realm and the large-scale digitization of previously existing analogue documents into digital formats, the traditional library approach was the only feasible one. There was simply no way to search millions of pages of printed text without actually reading them – and while reading a lot of books might be a very good way to gain command of a broad corpus of knowledge, it was not a reasonable way to find answers to specific questions. Thus, libraries performed an exceptionally important service to the world of scholarship by creating proxy records that allowed scholars and casual researchers alike to zero in quickly on those documents that might answer their questions or satisfy particular research needs. However, in an overwhelmingly digital information environment both the utility and the cost-effectiveness of proxy record creation are open to serious question. It has always been an extremely expensive and time-intensive strategy, one that relied heavily on the attention of a few highly trained librarians. In the print era the world of scholarship had little choice but to rely on librarians and their methods. In the digital era the world has moved very quickly past them.

In the 21st century, Google has effectively taken over the document-finding role from libraries. It was not very long ago that a researcher, when wondering what kinds of books might be available on the subject of Florentine sculpture, would have no real choice except to start her search with a library catalogue. No rational researcher would do so today, because a library catalogue will not answer the question effectively. She may find ten books on the subject in her library, but will not know whether more and better books exist elsewhere; she may find no books on the subject in her library, but will not know whether this means that no such books exist or simply that the library does not own any. The rational researcher will begin by searching as widely as possible, rather than within the artificially limited confines of any particular library catalogue. This may mean making a Google search; it may mean making a search on Amazon.com or on a similar bookselling site; in some cases it may mean making a search on a large online union catalogue such as WorldCat – but few researchers will think to look there, and those who do will still be left wondering whether the holdings of WorldCat's participant libraries really represent everything that is technically available.

Libraries – the crisis of the collection

When Google took over the searching and finding function from traditional libraries, it left one of the library's most essential functions fully intact: that of third-party broker for expensive, high-quality documents such as research journals and scholarly monographs. While the open web democratized access to facts, figures, popular articles and other casual research and ready-reference materials, access to more specialized content was still enjoyed only by those who could either afford to buy it themselves (an extremely rare few) or those who had access to extensive public libraries or academic research collections. Large collections of even relatively affordable documents, such as literary works or popular magazines, required huge amounts of storage space and significant organizational skill in order to make them accessible. As materials moved online and required less space and less externally imposed organization, they were still very expensive in the aggregate, and library budgets remained a crucial tool in making the materials available to those who needed access.

Then Google struck again. In late 2004 the company announced plans to digitize, on a massive scale, the full content of books from major research libraries throughout the Western world. Because of copyright restrictions, Google would not be able to make the complete contents of every book freely available to all – however, it did plan to make the contents of each book *fully searchable* by all, and excerpts available, subject to copyright limitations. This it proceeded to do, scanning and digitizing massive amounts of content from the libraries of Harvard, Princeton and Oxford universities, and the universities of Michigan, California and Virginia, among many others in an increasingly international and diverse group. By the end of 2008, over seven million titles – many of them previously available only to the very privileged few with access to these top-notch research collections – had been opened up to the search queries of anyone with access to the internet, and a significant minority of the titles in question were freely available to the public for online reading or printing (Drummond, 2008).

Libraries' response to the Google Book Search (GBS) juggernaut has, generally, been that of an ostrich that pauses, as it whistles past the graveyard, only long enough to stick its head in the sand. It is as if a manufacturer of carriages had responded to the development of the automobile by snorting that it may be faster, more economical and more comfortable than the horse-drawn carriage, but it still doesn't fly, does it? One of the first criticisms of GBS was that while it makes millions and millions of books searchable, most of those books are available for only very limited downloading, due to copyright restrictions. While this is true, it ignores a very important fact about the nature of research: even in the print realm, most of a research library's books are used, most of the time, like databases. The student carrying a pile of ten books out of the stacks and into a study carrel usually has no intention of reading those books from cover to cover, but intends, rather, to interrogate them, looking for relevant chapters, pages and passages. This he does, at great expense of time and energy, by using crude and ineffective indexes. GBS makes this variety of research immensely easier and quicker; even those books still under copyright can be searched freely, and extracts read, copied and cited. GBS does not make everything completely and freely available, but it makes a vast amount of material easily and quickly searchable, and vast tracts of it freely available – and does so far more completely, easily and freely than any individual library ever could. This fact is what will affect the future of the traditional library, and it is in this reality that the crisis of the collection consists.

Publishers – the crisis of price

Libraries have been warning for decades of a looming budget crisis. The genesis of this warning is both simple and undeniable: an inflation rate for many scholarly publications (particularly journals in the hard and social sciences) that has persisted at unsustainable levels for the past several decades. Libraries, over the same period, have seen their budgets increase at far lower rates (when they increase at all). There is no reason to believe that either of these trends will change in the foreseeable future.

This reality has two fundamental impacts on the scholarly information marketplace. First, libraries, saddled with rapidly increasing prices for ongoing access to journals to which they already subscribe, are able to buy smaller and smaller numbers of new subscriptions each year, when they are able to buy any at all. Second, and consequently, publishers find themselves able to sustain growth only at the expense of other publishers. In other words, the rate at which libraries infuse cash into the scholarly information environment has stalled, while publishers work with increasing desperation to steal shares of a shrinking market from each other. The crisis has been looming for decades, but its inevitable arrival was greatly hastened by a sharp and worldwide economic downturn in late 2008 and 2009. Libraries throughout the world saw budget cuts – in some cases disastrous ones – during this period, and in many cases the bulk of those cuts was absorbed by materials budgets. What has always been a fundamentally unsustainable situation has come to a head more quickly than many anticipated.

It is a situation that has resulted in much apocalyptic commentary, many calls for reform and little real change. There have been calls for sustainable business models and even for 'transformative' ones (University of California Office of Scholarly Communication, 2009), but so far relatively few models have proved to be both. The business models can basically be boiled down into three general categories: reader pays, author pays and the taxation model.

Reader pays

The most common model, and the one that is most clearly rational, is the one that requires readers to pay. What makes this model more rational than others is the simple fact that those who want access to a document are required pay for it, while those who do not want access are not charged. What makes the model objectionable, of course, is the fact that so many who do want access cannot afford it.

This leads to a major complicating factor in the discussion: the degree to which value-laden beliefs and empirically based quantitative factors become intertwined. Is the traditional, reader-pays subscription model itself broken and unsustainable, or is the model itself sound but the pricing patterns impossible to sustain? Which is fairer and better for society at large: for all to pay a small amount for access regardless of whether they want it, or for a few to pay a larger (and in some cases truly huge) amount for what they want and nothing for what they do not? And if the latter arrangement is deemed acceptable, how much should the customer have to pay?

Author pays

Under this model, costs that were borne by subscribers are shifted to the authors of research articles and access is then made freely available to the public. There is a certain undeniable logic to this approach: the scholarly information marketplace is largely supply-driven rather than demand-driven (new books on Welsh literature in the Elizabethan period, however valuable they may be in fact, are generally supplied by people who need to write them rather than demanded by customers anxious to read them), and it is generally anyone's guess whether the document in question will offer lasting good to the scholarly community beyond a basic salutary impact on the author's CV and career. If the most obvious benefit of publication is to the author, why should the author not foot the bill?

One obvious response is that the author will not, in the vast majority of cases, actually foot that bill. The money will come from his home institution or will be written into his grant proposal. One could argue that this simply shifts the costs around in a fundamentally irrational way, ensuring that scholarship that is destined to have little or no impact on the world will be supported as if it were important. On the other hand, the traditional subscription model has had exactly the same effect, requiring customers to buy many articles that they do not want in order to get access to the ones they do.

Taxation

The word 'taxation' is here used to describe any system that uses public money (whether in the form of actual taxes or of public granting-agency funds) to underwrite the free public distribution of research articles and similar documents that would otherwise be available only to subscribers. In practice, many 'author-pay' programmes are actually taxation programmes, since the money ultimately comes from public coffers.

The taxation model has a fundamental problem: it charges many, many people for access to the documents in question, regardless of how many of those people actually want or care about getting access. On the other hand, it spreads the cost very thinly, which means that the actual impact on any individual will be minimal. It can also be argued that while the average person may have little or no use for a paper on forensic histology, everyone in the world benefits when access to such papers is broadly available to those who do have a use for them.

Which of these three models should be implemented, and which of them is the fairest? Any question that begins with 'should' and includes the word 'fair' is going to be impossible to settle by quantitative or empirical argument. Publishers would generally like to price their titles based on the value that they perceive their products to be offering to the world; customers (particularly libraries) would like the products to be within reach for all and are generally suspicious of value-based pricing, even when they agree (and often they do not) with publishers' assessments of the objective value of their products. Since publishers have monopoly control of articles and books in which they hold copyright, they are in practice free to set prices according to their desires. This fact has led both to prices that are, in some cases, prohibitively high and to calls (some successful) for various kinds of government intervention. How this will all play out remains to be seen, although the movement towards mandated Open Access (OA) archiving had gained significant momentum by the end of 2008 (Cambridge University Library, 2009).

Sustainability of the subscription model

From a purely economic perspective, the subscription model is clearly sustainable; it has been sustained for centuries and did not begin to show cracks until prices began spiralling out of control. It is difficult to imagine that, if all scientific journals were priced at $15 per year and price increases never exceeded 1% annually, anyone would claim that the system was broken.

However, there is a more subtle sense in which the subscription model is less clearly sustainable. The journal subscription is a left-over artefact of the print era, when the constraints of physical printing and distribution made it necessary to bundle articles together and ship them out as issues. Identifying and individually purchasing only the articles one wanted was not practical, so in order to gain access to those articles one had no choice but to buy many articles one did not want as well. The online environment, in which printing is unnecessary and distribution can be virtually instantaneous, requires neither bundling nor the purchase of unwanted articles in order to get the articles one needs. The fact that we continue to accept the subscription model and the issue structure in this environment is puzzling, and cannot last. Eventually, subscribers will realize that a journal subscription means buying large amounts of content that is not wanted or needed and will refuse to subscribe. Budget cuts will only hasten this development.

This will (and arguably already does) pose a very difficult problem for journal publishers, who have for centuries depended on the sale of unwanted content to keep themselves afloat. This is not an indictment of publishers: in the print era, they had no choice but to sell unwanted content, partly because the economies of scale required it and partly because there was no way to anticipate which articles would be wanted by which subscribers. In the online era both publishers and their customers have been slow to realize that the purchase of unwanted content is no longer necessary. But it is nevertheless the case, and it is this fact more than any other that makes the current model of scholarly publication unsustainable: a system that works because its participants have not yet realized how poorly it serves them is a system that will fail sooner or later.

A new model for journals

What will take its place? It seems likely that while the journal will persist as a branding device (further discussion below), the idea of the journal *issue* is already moribund, and the subscription is soon to meet its demise. In an environment in which it is possible to show end-users everything that is available and charge them (or their broker agents) only for those items they want, it is difficult to believe that a wasteful and inefficient system like the subscription can continue to function.

What does seem to make sense is a system whereby a journal maintains a website on which articles are posted as soon as they are ready for distribution. The publisher would need to maintain a relatively steady stream of output in order to keep customers' interest, but there would be no reason to hold individual articles until a batch of them was ready – the articles could be posted one or two at a time. Each article would be individually dated and assigned a unique digital object identifier (DOI). End-users would be able to search the full content of all articles, but would be able to see only the full citation and abstract (plus, perhaps, a representative page or two of text) at no charge, and would pay for the right to download the full text – or perhaps pay a smaller fee to view the full text on screen and a larger fee to download and save a copy.

A system such as this would allow for the possibility of a 'subscription', which in this case would mean that a library or end-user would pay up front for the right to download everything published under the aegis of the journal. But it is difficult to see what would be gained by such an arrangement, since it is unlikely that every article published would be of sufficient interest to justify purchase. Much better would be to buy nothing until one had seen what was on offer, and then to buy only what was needed. Libraries could still act as brokers, making the per-article payment on behalf of the patron, who need never know that the desired article was not part of the library's 'collection' to begin with.

There is no reason why a system such as this could not work equally well for electronic books – and, with certain modifications, even for printed ones.

Evaluating and selecting resources in a mixed economic environment

The world of scholarly information is currently in a state of wild flux and confusion. The scholarly journal has been a fundamental tool of scholarship for centuries; however, the pricing crisis, a world economic meltdown and the OA insurgency have combined to make it very unclear in what form the traditional journal will endure. The scholarly monograph is, if anything, an even more venerable and basic scholarly commodity, and yet research libraries everywhere are seeing dramatic declines in their use, while the GBS project has created a massive online research library that is fully searchable by anyone with internet access. It is no longer clear to publishers to what degree access to information can still be sold to end-users at all.

One thing that GBS illustrates is that free/fee is no longer a true dichotomy. When the full text is searchable, and relevant (even if brief) passages are available for reading – and thus for citing – it may not matter that the entire document is not freely available for copying or download. This is not to say that the difference no longer matters, only that the line that separates 'free' from 'fee' is now quite a bit blurrier than it once was, and is likely to become more so.

This points to another thing that GBS makes clear, perhaps for the first time: the degree to which books in research libraries are used as databases rather than as documents for extended reading. This is not truly surprising – anyone who wrote research papers in college will recall the large numbers of books that he searched and consulted and cited without reading them from cover to cover – but it does clarify a long-standing dispute over the relative merits of print books and electronic books. The single most compelling argument against e-books has always been that they are not fit for extended reading. While few would dispute that point, it is also true that relatively few books in research libraries' print collections are ever subjected to linear, cover-to-cover reading, in any case. To the degree that they are, rather, searched for relevant chapters, pages or passages, books are being used as databases – regardless of their physical format. And to the degree that they are being used as databases they will be much more helpful to patrons in online formats than in print.

Libraries in the digital revolution

When information was primarily distributed in print formats, it was very important for libraries to create collections that were both as large and as carefully selected as possible. Since printed paper was expensive to produce and difficult to distribute, and since determining the very existence of books on particular topics could be an incredibly time-consuming chore, it was important that library patrons in search of documents should find these documents waiting for them when they arrived; procuring them after users' interest was known was a slow and inefficient process.

The digital revolution has completely changed this reality. Information still requires significant effort to be created in the first place, but once created it can be distributed easily, cheaply and in many cases instantaneously. Perhaps even more importantly, relevant documents are now much easier to locate and examine than they were when the only searching tools available were printed indexes that were always incomplete and out of date. Large-scale full-text searching now makes it possible for even inexpert searchers to zero in very quickly on documents that are relevant to their research needs. It is also worth noting that it is now very much easier to locate and purchase out-of-print books than it once was; no longer does the library have to jump on the university press monograph immediately upon publication in order to ensure that a copy will make it into the collection. Thanks to online aggregators like Bookfinder.com, ABE Books and Alibris, federated searching of many used-book dealers' holdings is now possible.

For libraries, then, the urgent and rather frightening question is this: in a world in which relevant books and articles can be located quickly and easily, where they can frequently be purchased online and access can be granted instantaneously, and where even print materials can be located and ordered with unprecedented ease and speed, what is the justification for purchasing large numbers of printed books and stockpiling them ahead of time against the by-no-means certain possibility of future patron need?

One answer to this question might be that the library is about more than simply meeting users' immediate needs; it is also about applying bibliographic wisdom to the creation of a wisely selected subset of the overwhelming universe of available documents. The problem is that our users seem to be decreasingly interested in taking advantage of that service. They tend to feel, rightly or wrongly, that they themselves are capable of evaluating and selecting the resources that will meet their needs, if only given the opportunity to do so. If entities other than the library give them that opportunity, they will take it. Library patrons may believe that they are just as good as librarians at evaluating and selecting research materials. But whether they are correct or not matters little to the future of libraries and publishers. The effect on members of the traditional scholarly information chain will be exactly the same – they will not survive.

Mobile devices and mobile access

It is an article of conventional faith that no one wants to read for extended periods from an electronic screen. This may be true, but it is probably time to revisit that particular piece of conventional wisdom, for at least two reasons:

1   Electronic screens are quickly becoming much more readable. The Kindle e-book reader, which features a screen made up of microscopic coloured balls that flip from black to white to form text, provides a reading surface that is every bit as easy on the eyes as printed paper (Amazon, 2009). The Kindle has drawbacks, of course: for one, it is like a book in that you have to remember to pick it up and take it with you; additionally, many still find the

navigation awkward. Navigation problems will fix themselves; the 'have to go out of my way to use it' factor will not.

2 Not all pleasure reading is extended reading. While it may indeed be uncomfortable to read for a two-hour stretch from an electronic screen, reading for 15 minutes is not. And as the iPhone and its quickly multiplying touch-screen imitators continue to take over the market, two things are quickly becoming increasingly possible: first, one can have a book (or two or three) tucked inconspicuously into one's pocket at all times; second, one can take it out and begin reading at any moment, and put it away again as soon as something else demands one's attention.

What currently exist in the e-book market, then, are two complementary but potentially powerful hardware tools: one (the Kindle) that allows the user to download very large numbers of books and read them comfortably for extended periods; another (the iPhone and its imitators) that allows the user to carry a few books around at all times and read them comfortably during brief and unanticipated moments of opportunity. Between the two, it is difficult to imagine that the e-book market is not at a major turning point – though it should be noted that prognosticators have been heralding the 'tipping point' for e-books for a very long time.

The future of the journal

While the journal seems likely to persist as a branding device, it is not likely to do so in its traditional format – 'format', in this case, referring to the standard volume/issue bundling of journal content rather than to physical manifestation. Up until now, e-journals have followed very closely the traditional volume/issue format that prevailed during the print era. But the traditional, three-layer format of journal publishing – articles compiled into issues compiled into volumes – has never been a rational one (as discussed above). It was forced upon us by the tyranny of ink on paper, which made it necessary for publishers to realize economies of scale as best they could. This meant constantly waiting: waiting for writers to finish writing, for editors to finish editing, for reviewers to finish reviewing, and then for enough finished articles to pile up that it was finally cost-effective to print, bind and mail the articles out in bundles.

Freed from that tyranny, there is no longer any need for journal publishers to hold back from publishing finished articles as soon as they have been reviewed and thoroughly prepared. Issues, frequency and numbering no longer matter. What continue to matter are the fact that a particular article was deemed worthy of publication by a particular journal, and the date on which it was published.

What the digital realm, with its relatively low barriers to publication, also allows us to do is to recognize different strata of scholarliness and give each one an equal treatment in the digital environment. This is both a blessing and a curse, and it actually reinforces the value of the journal brand. If a peer-reviewed research article is indistinguishable at first glance from an unreviewed opinion piece, then the imprimatur of an established journal's trusted editorial board becomes more important than ever to those who need quickly to identify papers that will likely be of high relevance and quality. At the same time, the scholarly world is enriched by the participation of a greater diversity of thinkers and by the presence of materials that would never have been distributed in print formats. Some of what finds its way into the conversation will be garbage, but much of it will be (and has already been shown to be) worthwhile.

Pre-print services

One specific threat to the traditional journal is the pre-print aggregator. Services such as the arXiv (a pre-print server designed specifically to facilitate access to raw data and preliminary research results) and the proliferating institutional repositories serve a different function from that of traditional peer-reviewed journals, but the two are not entirely complementary. Before such a thing as the arXiv was possible, the function that it now serves – the sharing of research information – was performed partly by informal exchange between individual scientists and partly by publication in formal journals. There were many scientists who would have benefited from having access to preliminary versions of papers but did not have the contacts necessary to take advantage of informal channels and therefore had to wait until the formal versions were published. Presumably, some of them would have been happy to make do with the informal versions for much if not all of the time. Those are the subscribers whom journal publishers risk losing to the arXiv and similar services. So far, it does not seem that these services are going to push formal journals out of the marketplace in any wholesale way, but publishers must be aware of their capability to erode the subscriber base.

Open Access

It is worth pointing out that OA, in its various manifestations, poses another threat to the traditional journal model. It is not that traditional journals *cannot* continue in an OA environment – ultimately, OA is just one pricing model among many, one that shifts the cost of a journal from the reader to some other party. However, the reality (at least so far) is that sustainable, long-term OA publishing models have yet to emerge. The Public Library of Science (PloS) uses 'bulk, cheap publishing of lower-quality papers' (Butler, 2008) to make possible the OA distribution of more serious work, and although OA publisher BioMed Central characterizes itself as 'pleasantly profitable' (Butler, 2008), it was sold to Springer in 2008 and its future business model remains in question. At the same time, various science, technical and medical publishers' attempts at creating OA options within the context of for-profit publishing (such as Springer's Open Choice programme) have yet to show much more than potential. In this environment, one in which the sustainability of OA is still very much in question, mandates such as those imposed by the National Institutes of Health (2008) in the USA and Research Councils UK (2006), not to mention those imposed internally by universities, may force the scholarly literature to breathe air that cannot sustain it. If a professor whose university imposes a hard OA mandate wishes to publish in a journal that does not allow free public distribution of its articles, that professor is prevented from doing so. There are good arguments to be made in favour of such a policy. On the other hand, limiting an author's publication options in such a way will also entail costs and consequences, not all of them intentional. One likely consequence is a greater difficulty for journal publishers. How great will the difficulty become? It is much too soon to say, but it is worth keeping in mind.

Institutional repositories

Institutional repositories (IRs) pose another threat to traditional journal publishing. Unlike the arXiv, an IR is intended to showcase, preserve and distribute access to the final products of locally supported research. These aims intrude directly on the goal of a traditional journal. It is certainly possible to manage the conflict so that both sides continue to benefit – access to an article in the IR might be embargoed temporarily, for example, in order to allow a journal to publish first and be a sole resource for some period of time. But growing numbers of research institutions are requiring their faculty members to deposit all of their work in the local IR in final, published versions, and to do so at the point of publication rather than following an embargo period. To the degree that such mandates grow in number and influence, and that research institutions' repositories grow and become highly used, it seems likely that the environment for traditional publishers will at least become much more complex and will very likely become substantially more difficult as well. The result for the larger scholarly information environment will be, it seems safe to say, mixed.

The pricing crisis

Journal pricing strategies and library budgets have been on a collision course for decades. For as long as journal price increases have outstripped library budget increases, it has been clear that the situation was unsustainable; however, innovative selling strategies such as the Big Deal have allowed individual publishers to keep the wolf of budget constraints temporarily at bay while also locking customers into contractual commitments that preclude the natural winnowing that comes from the cancellation of unpopular titles.

There are several possible solutions to the pricing crisis:

1 Publishers decide to accept a rate of price increase that matches their customers' rate of budget increase.
2 Scholarly publishing is removed entirely from the market sector and effectively nationalized.
3 The traditional subscription model of publishing, which forces subscribers to purchase articles they do not want in order to get articles they do want, is replaced by affordable single article purchasing.

4 OA becomes so predominant that virtually all costs are shifted away from end-users and on to some blend of taxpayers, third-party donors and sponsoring institutions. (Depending on how the blend plays out, this could turn out to be essentially the same as scenario 2, with the additional participation of private foundations and sponsors.)

None of these solutions is obvious on the near-term horizon, and none of them would be straightforward or easy. All would entail unanticipated consequences, just as the current system does. It is probably too late for publishers to change their pricing practices dramatically; shareholders are not notable for their understanding of the complex realities of the scholarly information marketplace. Nationalization is always fraught with complication and unforeseen consequences, and (it must be said) frequently with bureaucratic incompetence. Purchasing individual articles is a fundamentally rational way of distributing access to journal content, but in itself it does not actually address the pricing problem – at $30 or $40 per download, such purchasing of many journals' content would be even less affordable than a subscription. A large-scale OA solution remains elusive, in part because of a recalcitrant academic culture that has not yet learned how to deal with non-traditional publishing options, and in part because OA amounts to a cost-shifting project and there is as yet no consensus on where exactly the costs should end up.

What is clear is that the crisis point is suddenly much closer, much sooner than anyone expected. Libraries that have sustained double-digit cuts to their materials budgets (and as of this writing in early 2009, that cohort is very large) are making extremely difficult decisions about how to cut their subscription profiles for 2010–11 and are planning to have to make similarly difficult decisions for the following year. It seems very likely that, ten years from now, we will be looking back at 2010–11 as the year that the serials pricing crisis finally came to a head.

Conclusion – scholarly information on the near horizon

Prognostication is, famously, a sucker's game. However, there are some current trends that, it seems wise to assume, will form a permanent part of the future scholarly information landscape, and there are some coming developments that seem inevitable. Some of these have been discussed in more detail above.

Open Access

The OA movement generated considerable momentum between 2005 and 2009, and will continue to grow in significance and influence. What remains to be seen is whether and to what degree it will actually displace traditional publication, or whether it will simply create a new niche in the scholarly communication marketplace. Given the manifest difficulty of incorporating OA practices into existing, traditional publishing models, it seems likely that the only way OA will displace the traditional avenues of publication will be if tenure and promotion practices and standards change substantially. While that is likely to happen eventually, it seems unlikely that it will happen within the next decade.

Commercial education/training programmes

Although it takes a great deal of specialized knowledge to teach upper-division and graduate-level coursework in most scientific and technical disciplines, it is by no means clear that such knowledge is needed to teach introductory courses. It is very possible that introductory college coursework will be taken over by entities (some of them commercial) that are willing to administer it in a more efficient and results-oriented manner than most colleges and universities can or wish to do; to some degree this has happened already, particularly in the USA. To the degree that this phenomenon grows, it will exert a mighty change on colleges and universities, which will become even more specialized, and more focused on research rather than on instruction. We should be on the lookout for such developments now: economic crisis leads to more, not less, demand for this kind of training and instruction, as members of the workforce feel a greater need to sharpen and certify their skills and as the opportunity cost of education drops.

Pricing implosion

The economic crisis is hastening the point at which libraries will be required finally to deal in a strategic and programmatic way with the unsustainability of current journal pricing. Large shareholder-owned science publishers, which have heretofore depended on both market cannibalism and exorbitant inflation rates to maintain annual revenue growth, will hit the wall in terms of subscription pricing and will branch out into new kinds of information products (possibly leaving formal journal publishing to non-profit entities). There are hints of such efforts already under way.

Mission change in academic and research libraries

Public libraries will continue to serve the general functions that are their current stock-in-trade: supporting the school work of students aged 5–18, and providing pleasure reading for the general public. Research libraries, however, will change dramatically over the next decade. Much of their role as repositories of standard research collections will have been obviated by a combination of GBS and the decline of librarian-crafted collections. The demise of the research collection will be hastened by the financial crisis that began in 2007 and will persist in some degree for years to come. The coming decade will be a difficult one for academic libraries. During this period, institutions of higher learning will be forced to confront and deal with the radical wastefulness inherent in traditional models of collection development and will turn to more efficient, patron-centred and patron-driven acquisition models. A few major research libraries will continue to serve as monumental collections that represent the totality of Western intellectual culture, while the vast majority will tighten their focus on serving the real-time needs of their specific patron populations and on capturing and giving the world access to locally produced scholarship, locally produced data sets and the rare and unique materials that would otherwise not be captured by the system of commercial scholarship.

Book publishing

By the end of the coming decade, the concept of 'out of print' will have become a quaint memory. No document that has its origins as a digital file need ever become unavailable to those who wish to purchase it. In a related development, most books will be printed and bound only on demand. The technology for implementing such a programme already exists, and its clear superiority to traditional mass printing and speculative distribution will push the old distribution methods out of the mainstream of the marketplace fairly quickly. While blockbuster novels and popular nonfiction will continue to be printed on a just-in-case basis for some time to come, everything at the margins (which comprises the vast majority of published output) will be printed only as needed, when needed.

Journal publishing

Journal titles will become brands with which to identify high-quality articles rather than actual serial publications; the concept of a 'journal issue' will be relegated to the past. This development may take longer than the shift from speculative to on-demand book printing but it is inevitable, for many of the same reasons. Traditional journal publishing will also feel an impact from an inevitable shift in promotion and tenure standards, though this will take even longer. In 2009 there are still members of university faculties who do not understand that there is no necessary difference in quality and rigour between printed and online peer-reviewed journals. This problem is largely generational and will be remedied by retirements over the next decade; what will take longer will be the establishment of updated standards that will allow tenure committees to evaluate non-standard publication formats and venues.

References

Amazon (2009) *Kindle: wireless reading device*,
    www.amazon.com/gp/B0015T963C [accessed 4 November 2009].
Blachman, N. and Peek, J. (2007) *Google Search Engine Results Pages (SERPs)*,
    www.googleguide.com/results_page.html [accessed 4 November 2009].
Butler, D. (2008) PloS Stays Afloat with Bulk Publishing, *Nature*, 2 July, 454, 11,
    www.nature.com/news/2008/080702/full/454011a.html [accessed 4 November 2009].
Cambridge University Library (2009) *About Open Access*,
    www.lib.cam.ac.uk/create_change [accessed 4 November 2009].
Drummond, D. (2008) New Chapter for Google Book Search, *The Official Google Blog*, 28 October,

http://googleblog.blogspot.com/2008/10/new-chapter-for-google-book-search.html [accessed 4 November 2009].

National Institutes of Health (2008) *Revised Policy on Enhancing Public Access to Archived Publications Resulting from NIH-funded Research*, http://publicaccess.nih.gov/policy.htm.

Panitch, J. M. and Michalak, S. (2005) *The Serials Crisis: a white paper for the UNC-Chapel Hill Scholarly Communications Convocation*, www.unc.edu/scolcomdig/whitepapers/panitch-michalak.html [accessed 4 November 2009].

Research Councils UK (2006) *Research Councils UK's Updated Position Statement on Access to Research Outputs*, www.rcuk.ac.uk/cmsweb/downloads/rcuk/documents/2006statement.pdf [accessed 4 November 2009].

University of California Office of Scholarly Communication (2009) *Support Publishing Experiments and New Business Models*, http://osc.universityofcalifornia.edu/sustainable/new_business_models.html [accessed 4 November 2009].

3

Scholarly communications: the publisher's view

Ian Russell

Background

For the future of digital information to be orderly, that information must be discoverable, accessible, structured, interoperable, linked, semantically tagged and well identified; it must have clear provenance and good version control; and it must be preserved and curated. There must also be a means of bestowing authority on the corpus of literature in order to give the readers a quick but effective way of assessing the importance or likely importance of anything that they come across. Nowadays it needs to embrace both formal and informal scholarly communications (to include not only scholarly journals and monographs but also blogs, wikis, tweets and whatever else web users throw at it). And, of course, all this needs to have a sustainable and robust funding mechanism behind it and to be scalable to deal with the ever-increasing outputs from scholarship.

There is no doubt whatsoever in my mind that the future of digital scholarly information will be orderly. Research efficiency depends on it and is something that will be increasingly scrutinized as funders and research establishments look to maximize the impact of the research that they are associated with. For the most part, the academy will also demand organization, although there are currently widespread instances where academics act in their individual interests rather than for the collective benefit of scholarship, for example by storing data only on un-networked computers in their labs. The question, then, is how we get to this orderly future. What barriers are in the way and what obstacles need to be overcome? How can we get to that future as quickly as possible, taking the best of the present with us instead of destroying something now only to reinvent it later?

I am going to restrict myself primarily to a discussion of scientific journal publishing since that is what I know best, but much of what follows is, or will become, applicable to other disciplines. Indeed the issues of discoverability, digital curation and preservation, version control, provenance and trustworthiness are applicable to all online content, including scholarly e-books, research data, audio and video files, news content, etc. In the discussion that follows, I will use the NISO Journal Article Version recommended practice nomenclature for article versions, a full explanation of which can be found in NISO (2008) .

Drivers for change

If scholarly publishing has not undergone a revolution since the mid 1990s, it has certainly undergone a sustained period of intensive evolution. In many ways journal publishing has been a model industry in terms of the adoption of new technology, and academic publishers have embraced the web in a way that few other industries have.

Online delivery

The moves to e-mail correspondence, online submission systems and web-based tools to facilitate peer review and manuscript tracking have greatly speeded up the publication process, and these practical innovations and improvements will continue. However, the online delivery of content is perhaps the most visible result of the adoption of internet technologies. In 1995, when the web was still in its infancy, a handful of journals were available online via rudimentary interfaces – if you had the patience to download them (even the academic networks were painfully slow back then).

Spool forward ten years to 2005, by which time 93% of the journals in science, technology and medicine (STM) and 84% of arts, humanities and social science (AHSS) journals were available online (Cox and Cox, 2005). By 2008, 96% of STM and 87% of AHSS journals were online (Cox and Cox, 2008) and they were being delivered by sophisticated interfaces which had begun to take the research article beyond a mere facsimile of the printed page, and to allow linking through to multimedia, online datasets and other supplementary material. These can mash up and re-present data from a variety of sources. This is all the more impressive when you consider that about half of the world's journals are published by society publishers and, of these, over 97% publish three or fewer journals, with almost 90% publishing just one title (Crow, 2006).

Open Access

There are other outside influences too. Funders and research institutions are wishing to exert more influence over the research that they are associated with, and this has led to a number of Open Access (OA) mandates of various kinds. There is also a powerful, well funded OA lobby that benefits from emotive arguments, and this in turn has led to support from governments – particularly those without a publishing industry – supporting calls for free access to research without, perhaps, fully understanding all of the implications. In general, though, researchers, to the annoyance of the OA lobbyists and as evidenced by the low take-up of OA publishing and self-archiving, are happy with the established system.

Why is this? Perhaps they understand – possibly more than the publishers themselves – the value that publishers add in dealing with things like information overload.

Information overload

Early journal publishing

Information overload is nothing new; it has been an issue since the beginning of modern scholarly endeavour. Early scholarly communication relied on the exchange of letters between intellectuals, but the first scholarly journals to emerge in Europe, *Journal des Sçavans* and *Philosophical Transactions*, both first published in 1665, collated accounts of interesting observations and discoveries and circulated these to a much wider audience.

Peer review began in *Philosophical Transactions*, published by the Royal Society, as an attempt by Henry Oldenburg (the Society's first Secretary, and editor and publisher of the journal) to select interesting accounts. Oldenburg's selection, backed by the weight of the Royal Society, helped those with an interest in the emerging field of natural philosophy (which we would now call science) by providing both improved access and a quality selection. As journals evolved throughout the Enlightenment period, they did much to promote the ideas of evidence-based science and reason and helped to challenge existing dogmas. Many journals of the time mostly published book reviews, but for scholars they helped greatly to sift the already large quantity of reading material available. However, information overload was clearly still an issue, some 160 years after the first issue of *Philosophical Transactions* was published, as eloquently noted by Michael Faraday:

> It is certainly impossible for any person who wishes to devote a portion of his time to chemical experiment, to read all the books and papers that are published in connection with his pursuit; their number is immense, and the labour of winnowing out the few experimental and theoretical truths which in many of them are embarrassed by a very large proportion of uninteresting matter, of imagination, and of error, is such that most persons who try the experiment are quickly induced to make a selection in their reading, and thus inadvertently, at times, pass by what is really good. (Faraday, 1826)

Chinese research output in the 21st century

Despite the increasing specialization in academic endeavour, a highly developed network of journals and great technological advances in search and discovery, information overload is still a growing issue today. Increasing research outputs from China will prove an additional challenge. The Chinese government has been investing heavily in the funding of basic research, with research and development funding tripling in the ten years from 1998 to 2008. There are plans for a further four-fold increase by 2020, and universities and research centres the length and breadth of China boast brand new buildings filled with state-of-the-art equipment.

Also there is a 'returning tide' (Wells, 2007) of Chinese scholars who have trained in Western universities, and they are bringing with them best-of-breed methods which are boosting the quality and effectiveness of Chinese research. In addition, a step change is occurring in the command of English. Reversal of the prohibition on learning English that was imposed during the Cultural Revolution and that created a barrier to the publication of Chinese work in international (predominantly English language) journals will eliminate the language barrier for 21st-century Chinese scholars. By 2003 English was compulsory in Chinese schools, and now more than 10 million elementary school pupils and 60 million high school students are learning English. According to Wang Ying (2007), more than 200 million Chinese were learning English in 2007.

The impact of these changes is already being seen. Chinese research output in ISI-ranked[1] journals has been doubling every five years since 1980 and currently stands at over 100,000 papers (roughly the same as in the UK), and the total number of citations to these articles and the average cites per paper are also increasing rapidly. In the near future, as a result of increased R&D expenditure, the returning tide of Chinese academics, Western research methods and the disappearing language barrier, we can expect a truly dramatic increase in the quantity, quality and impact of Chinese research. Many observers believe that India is around five years behind China.

The scholarly communication system is going to struggle to absorb this material, both in terms of paying for it (under either a subscription business model or any emerging new model) and in terms of the academy dealing with a huge increase in material. It seems obvious that researchers need more and better ways of determining what to read first and of being guided to trustworthy information – surely the *raison d'être* of publishers and librarians alike.

Provenance on the web

We all know that the internet has revolutionized the dissemination of information. The world wide web has made it possible for an amateur to make content available to a huge potential audience quickly, conveniently, without any particular specialist knowledge or skill and at a cost which, while not zero, is within easy reach of most. While publishing professionally does incur additional costs, the point remains valid that the barrier to entry has been dramatically reduced.

This, of course, is largely a good thing, but the relatively modest cost of publishing online does mean that a raft of incorrect, incoherent and sometimes deliberately misleading material (see for example Krane, 2006) appears on the web.

The provenance of what we find on the web is therefore of great importance. If you are searching for information on a particular cancer drug, for instance, you are likely to attach different import to what you find depending on whether you are reading information from the pharmaceutical company that produced it, a competing company, a patient support group, a cancer charity, a supporter of alternative therapy, etc. That is, if you know where the information you are finding comes from. What is needed is an easily identifiable, trustworthy resource – a brand which you recognize and with which you associate credibility.

Formal publication processes

It has been argued (Roosendaal and Geurts, 1997) that formal publication can be viewed as four functions, namely, registration (establishing precedence and intellectual priority), certification (certifying quality), awareness (ensuring accessibility of research) and archiving (preserving research for future use). It is important to note that certification includes 'selection', and I would argue that 'awareness' should actually be split into two functions: discoverability (making sure research can be found) and dissemination (making research available). It should be noted that Roosendaal and Geurts' functions are integrated in journal publishing, but many commentators (see for example Van de Sompel et al., 2004) have observed that they could be disaggregated into independent, discrete services.

What Roosendaal and Geurts refer to as 'concrete functions', namely certification and awareness, form a mechanism for bestowing authority on the corpus of literature, and thus help to deal with information overload.

Certification

Given the amount of material available, a means of providing selection and authority is essential for a functional system, no matter how sophisticated our search and discovery (see below) tools become. In the scholarly environment, certification is most usually associated with peer review, but for the certification process to be effective it needs to be more than a binary process – something whereby a paper has either passed peer review or not. It needs to give readers a measure of the likely importance of a given piece of information. Currently in many (but by no means all) disciplines, a combination of peer review and journal brand provides this authority.

The association with a journal brand is important and makes peer review more than a mere binary process. The same peer reviewers could well accept a manuscript for one journal but reject it for another, based on the quality standards of the journal, its subject coverage or niche, the support of a particular doctrine, etc. The reviewers know what is acceptable for a particular journal (which is why it can be so hard for journal publishers to change their quality standards) and, similarly, readers get a great deal of information about an article by virtue of its association with a particular journal before they even read a word. Of course, the readers do not know from the journal title whether an article is good, bad or indifferent, but they do have an indication of what they are likely to find, and that is a very important filter on the literature. It is why authors posting to online repositories are so keen to associate their articles with a journal.

In the scholarly publishing environment this trustworthiness currently comes from the brand of the journal or the book publisher. The publisher takes responsibility for the credibility (not necessarily the correctness) of what it publishes. Some mechanism by which readers can quickly determine the credibility and trustworthiness of what they find online is a prerequisite for an orderly digital world, although of course this mechanism may not always be the established system of reliance on publisher brands.

Awareness – dissemination

In the days of print on paper, making content available was an expensive business. Thanks to Johannes Gutenberg and movable type, academics did not have to rely on monks copying scholarly works by hand, but typesetting, printing and distribution were still a costly exercise that needed expertise and expensive equipment.

Online digital publishing has changed all that, of course. Now dissemination, at least as far as 'making available' goes, is the easy and inexpensive part of the process. Some have replicated this function, looking to eliminate the costs of publishers, but they have misunderstood the function of making available as the primary purpose of publishers; it is not. We really do not have to worry about 'making available' in our quest for an orderly system of digital information.

Registration – an aside

As an aside, Roosendaal and Geurts' *registration* function is 'already fully matured' in the electronic environment, and in fact any trustworthy third party can fulfil the function of registering intellectual priority. Registration does, though, need to be tied to certification, and obviously is related to version. In journals, registration is by means of the date of submission, acceptance or publication, with the publicly available Version of Record being fixed at that point, though in some online journals changes can be made to the article and most journals have processes and procedures to publish errata, corrigenda, addenda, comments and replies.

Nonetheless, the publisher takes responsibility for the registration of a version of the article at a fixed point. In cases of disputes, publishers usually retain previous versions of the article, reviewer comments and correspondence with the authors, so that complaints can be investigated and resolved. Less formal publication media, like online repositories, could (and already do in some fields) perform the registration function, and here it is important that they determine, implement and manage policies to take responsibility for that function and have mechanisms for resolving disputes.

Awareness – discovery

The digital era has changed the way in which readers find content. It is not so long ago that academics would visit the library regularly to browse the latest literature. I have heard countless anecdotes from professors who stumbled across an important paper serendipitously while browsing a journal looking for something else, although these may be apocryphal or their importance exaggerated. Nonetheless, there is a general trend towards searching and away from browsing, and this raises a *bone fide* question: does this harm scholarship?

Search

When journals first found themselves on the web, publishers invested serious money in their content delivery platforms, pursuing the holy grail of making their websites 'sticky' – ensuring that visitors stayed on the site and were encouraged to come back regularly. I worked for a major physics publisher at that time and the hope was to build a website that would be the first port of call each day for any physicists worth their salt. To do this, we built great search functionality, we invented (I believe) reference linking and we came up with a plethora of personalized functions. But our readers and Google had other ideas.

Researchers, in the main, just did not want to work that way. They understandably wanted a one-stop shop, and Google gave them the facility to search a broad swathe of the literature. Almost overnight the focus changed. Instead of personalized functions, we were working on search-engine optimization. Instead of focusing on journal home pages, we were thinking about article abstract pages, because those were where users searching on Google were landing. So abstract pages suddenly contained better navigation and links to news and announcements and to other search and discovery tools, and we paid much more attention to branding at the article level; the unit was no longer the journal issue, let alone the volume – it was the article.

Publishers have to expose the full text of their articles to search engines for indexing. Not to do so is to miss out on an important avenue of traffic, although still today I hear of organizations (not established publishers) trying to build those sticky websites and refusing to allow Google to index them because they want direct traffic and not referrals from search engines. In most if not all cases, this is folly and doomed to failure; it is not what users want.

However, search engines index so much content that, even with sophisticated search behaviour, finding what you want can be like looking for the proverbial needle in a haystack, particularly if you only have incomplete information on what you are looking for. The trouble with text-based searching is that if you are searching, for example, for information using the word 'pipe', you will also find something that says 'this is not a pipe' (with apologies to René Magritte). The search engine does not understand the context of the words.

The semantic web

The web as we know it today pretty much follows a traditional print model, i.e. journals are broken down into volumes, issues and articles, and books into chapters. It is very much a web of documents existing within distinct data silos, with limited connections between documents. This makes it harder to find relevant, trustworthy material quickly and easily as more and more information becomes available via the web.

In contrast, the semantic web offers an array of opportunities to enhance the content-discovery and research process within scholarly publishing. The semantic web is an interconnected, integrated web of data allowing researchers to follow lines of research without having to resort to wading through pages and pages of search results, which may or may not have relevance to their research.

If we take citations as a conceptual example, we know that documents B and C cite document A, but within the world of the semantic web additional information can be stored about the relationships between citations, e.g. that document B supports document A but document C refutes A. This concept can be taken a step further by the addition of richer relationship layers between data, which could include:

- links to other papers written by the cited author(s), allowing users easily to navigate to other papers of interest
- concepts extracted from papers (ontologies, taxonomies and controlled vocabularies play an important part here), allowing users to drill down to concepts of interest and quickly see a definition of a key term, papers, chapters and raw datasets relevant to that concept, and so on
- relevant external datasets pulled in from trusted external resources, allowing users to review and manipulate raw research data and potentially to do further research in the field as a result – mash-ups or 'lively data' (Shotton, 2009; Shotton et al., 2009) are a good example of this
- links to research projects currently under way, author blogs, news items, etc.

The semantic web thereby builds an ever-expanding web of interconnecting data to support:

- further research and new discoveries
- cross-disciplinary collaboration resulting in richer applications
- increased visibility of relevant data
- ability for untrained researchers to find data quickly
- easier research collaboration
- a more interactive user experience.

It may well be that the semantic web has been over-hyped, but there is little doubt that it is beginning to gain momentum and has the potential to revolutionize the discovery process. Within the scholarly publishing space, the early adopters are leading the way with more widespread take-up expected to follow. More generally, the Obama administration has recently announced support for semantic-web technologies for datasets produced by the US government, the Google Rich Snippets project shows Google dipping its toes in the water of semantic-web technologies, and Elsevier's Grand Challenge offers researchers financial incentives to prototype tools dealing with the ever-increasing amount of online life-sciences information.

Alerting services

Publishers do a great deal to aid discovery. Search engine optimization (SEO) is big business; abstracting and indexing services have historically been important, but now their relevance and expense are being called into question. Other advances have already changed the way that academics work: e-mail alerts and RSS feeds of new material and tables of contents can be highly tailored across a number of journals and other services; these are delivered automatically to provide academics with what is, in effect, a personal journal. In addition, Web 2.0 technologies are facilitating the sharing of information between users.

Metadata and social bookmarking

Social bookmarking and social citation tools and services like del.icio.us (now Delicious),[2] CiteULike,[3],Connotea[4] and Diigo[5] are playing an increasingly important role in discovery. They allow users to tag content and share links and citations, adding metadata and creating 'folksonomies' – user-generated taxonomies – as they go. Implementing taxonomies has two major difficulties: (1) it is very labour intensive, and thus expensive, and (2) rigid taxonomies tend to lag behind the subjects that they are trying to categorize, especially in fast-moving fields. In the generation of folksonomies, the effort is distributed across the users, which, in addition to spreading costs, also means that categorization can evolve more quickly. Of course, the downside is a lack of control over the taxonomy.

Data and text mining

Perhaps the most important leap forward in the discovery process will come not from the interaction between humans and computers but from computer–computer interactions in the form of text and data mining. Allowing computers to trawl and analyse the literature will reveal latent facts: for example, previously unrecognized relationships between genes or drug interactions.

Success in this area will require the entire literature to be exposed to text and data mining, and results may be improved by content enrichment, the emergence of semantic standards, etc. Exposing the literature to mining could be achieved under an OA publishing model (see later), by publishers licensing material, or by their voluntarily exposing text and data in a machine-readable form for mining.

Challenges of stewardship

Data

There has been a disappointing lack of engagement regarding data among most stakeholders in the scholarly communication chain, and this includes academics, research institutions, librarians and publishers.

So-called 'big science' projects – the very large experiments like the Large Hadron Collider – have data storage and stewardship built into their core design, and are well catered for. However, the situation for bench science is very different and much more chaotic. Most publishers have the facility to store datasets alongside research texts but, with a few notable exceptions like the Organisation for Economic Co-operation and Development, they have done little to encourage authors to submit data and less to link data with the primary research literature.

The result is that information is being lost and the job of the researcher hindered. Take as one example a spectrum appearing in a journal article. Researchers still routinely print and enlarge graphs and then measure – with a ruler – the peaks on the spectrum, whereas if the graph were linked to the underlying dataset the researcher could get precise information at the click of a mouse.

Preservation and curation

In the print-on-paper world publishers did not have to worry much about the archiving and preservation of the material that they produced. Although *archiving* was one of the functions of formal publication mentioned by Roosendaal and Geurts (1997) and journals record the 'minutes of science', to use the phrase famously coined by Jan Velterop (1995), the physical archiving and responsibility for preserving the print-on-paper product was done by those who had bought the physical copy. It was bliss for the publishers, but the libraries had to invest in ever-larger amounts of shelf and archive space, and in climate-controlled, fire- and waterproof storage facilities for rare material.

Preservation and curation of digital material is going to be expensive, especially if your brief is to preserve something in perpetuity; for ever is a long time. In the print-on-paper world, preservation and archiving costs were mostly borne by the customer and duplicated many times over, and for good reason; local copies are needed for access by the locals. The cost of each instance of preservation is also readily justified, and the benefit is rendered obvious by a visit to the library shelves. The fact that duplication provides back-up, should a catastrophe strike and one copy be lost, is a bonus.

The digital world is different. For usage, in theory only one networked copy of a resource is needed, which everyone with an internet connection can access. More than one copy is needed for preservation – we need to keep at least as many copies as are required to guarantee that they cannot all be lost simultaneously in some catastrophic event. The 1s and 0s that make up digital information are much more ephemeral than trusty paper and ink; storage media degrade over time, and so effort must be expended to ensure the integrity of the digital file and correct any errors that arise. But the archiving of digital material must go beyond preserving the bits and bytes of the digital file. Digital curation, defined as 'the actions needed to maintain digital research data and other digital materials over their entire life-cycle and over time for current and future generations of users' (Digital Curation Centre, undated) is a huge problem and likely to be an extremely expensive one to solve. You can preserve a digital object, but it is much less useful if you do not know what or where it is, and it is utterly useless if you do not have the hardware and software needed to read it.

A number of initiatives have emerged, including those of private organizations (the best known examples are Portico and LOCKSS) and of national deposit libraries (for example e-Depot from the Koninklijke Bibliotheek), but the problem has not been solved yet and, although the role that publishers have to play in digital curation is an open question, the solution will require the commitment and involvement of all stakeholders.[6]

A particular issue in scholarly publishing is the preservation of material produced by the plethora of very small publishers that characterizes the scholarly publishing landscape. These organizations are the least likely to interact with formal archiving schemes and yet, because of their small size and often fragile finances, are probably producing the content that is most at risk.

Version control

The role of the journal as the archive is arguably being eroded; or at least, the online-only journal gives us the facility for a journal article to become a living, changing thing which can be corrected, updated and enhanced.

In addition, the ease with which material can be posted to the world wide web means that a variety of different versions appear, ranging from the Author's Original manuscript, through various intermediate versions produced by either the author or the publisher, to the Version of Record. The issue of version control is therefore a serious one.

It is vital that the scholarly journal literature is well defined. Currently, articles appearing in a journal are, in a sense, fixed in time, with the publisher taking responsibility for them and for making available a definitive version, the Version of Record; and while errata, corrigenda and addenda may be published subsequently, the Version of Record itself does not change. There can only be one version of the 'minutes of science' and there has to be a mechanism for taking responsibility for version control in general and for the definitive version of a work in particular.

Standards and interoperability

You may not think of standards as being very exciting; frankly, standards are not very exciting, but they are very important. The landscape of digital information is complex, and standards are needed for integration and interoperability. Try to imagine a telephone system, or indeed the internet itself, with no standards. It would be impossible, as no distributed system could work.

Someone has to develop and maintain these standards and, like everything else, this needs to be paid for.

Linking and the persistence of links

Thanks to CrossRef,[7] hypertext linking between research articles is now commonplace and readers have a new way of browsing the literature; for the first time they can bounce from one article to the next. Linking will become ever more pervasive and we are already seeing the facilitating technology behind this linking functionality, the digital object identifier (DOI), being assigned to book chapters, tables, charts, datasets, video and other forms of content.

Through linking, the formal scholarly literature will become ever more entwined with informal communication like blogs and wikis, and here the ephemeral nature of the web will become an increasing issue.

Currently, links from reference lists usually benefit from brand association with a journal or other publication, although links directly out from the full text to a cited resource may not. But, as linking becomes more widespread to encompass more types of information, there will need to be mechanisms that will indicate the nature of the cited resource and give the reader an indication of its provenance.

To sum up, the web will need a new service or group of services which will assign authority to links, and also check that they are not broken.

Costs

Unfortunately, the advent of the web has not made the process of scholarly publishing less expensive. Publishers have been able to realize substantial cost savings through a move away from traditional typesetting to electronic origination, either due to greater use of authors' electronic files, because the activity can be off-shored easily, or both. However, while it is possible to make content available online very inexpensively, professional publishers will tell you that the costs associated with sophisticated content delivery platforms, backfile digitization, reference linking, search optimization, storage, XML workflows, preservation, bandwidth, etc., are not trivial and have been a substantial additional cost over and above print production – particularly for the early adopters, when the technology was immature and costs were consequentially higher.

Publishers report that a significant number of libraries still require print copies of the journals they purchase, although in a 2009 Association of Learned and Professional Society Publishers survey (Russell, 2009) 91% of respondents wanted to move more material to electronic only. The main reasons cited for retaining print are concerns over perpetual access, continued demand from faculty and, in the developing world, a lack of ICT infrastructure.

However, the biggest reason given is that publishers do not offer electronic-only access, and that is because of the issue of VAT. Although VAT regimes in Europe vary, in the UK print journals attract zero-rated VAT while electronic journals attract VAT at the full rate. Thus electronic-only access is considerably more expensive than purchasing print alone or print and electronic combined. There is a 'catch 22' here, and it is an issue that must be addressed as a matter of urgency, because it is a prerequisite for a move to many of the emerging business models and would allow for very considerable system-wide cost savings. However, a move to online only is not good news for everyone;. In the newspaper world a case study by Thurman and Myllylahti (2009) showed that, for subscription-based online newspapers, while costs fell by 50%, online readership declined by 22% and revenue fell by 75%. Nonetheless, for the vast majority of scholarly publishers the transition will be a relatively easy and welcome one.

While the costs of print distribution vary with circulation (and so the more print subscriptions that are converted to electronic, the lower the distribution costs), much of the cost of producing print is a 'first copy cost', which means that publishers will not make real savings until they can eliminate print production altogether. However, most of the savings of a move to exclusively electronic provision – estimated to amount to £983 million per year globally (RIN, 2008) – will be accrued on the library side, due to the reduction of costs relating to shelving and reshelving, stack maintenance, checking in and out and physical storage space.

The serials crisis

It is often noted that the prices of subscription journals are increasing above the rate of inflation. There are two important points to make in respect of this statement. Firstly, so called 'big deals' (discounted packages of large numbers of journal titles) and consortia sales mean that many subscriptions are sold at a substantially discounted rate, particularly those from the large commercial publishers, who are often the subject of criticism regarding pricing. Secondly, global research and development budgets have been increasing at a rate of around 3–4% per year since the 1980s and there is a strong correlation between this, the number of researchers and research outputs in the form of journal articles (Mabe and Amin, 2001). This leads inexorably to an increase in the number of active journals and journals that are growing – the former showing a remarkably consistent rate of growth of around 3.5% since around the year 1700 (Mabe, 2003). The result is that for most established journals the price per article is falling, and is often a fraction of what it was even a decade ago.

Nonetheless, library budgets have failed to keep pace with increasing outputs. Current levels of availability have never been higher – a testament to the library and publishing communities working together – but libraries still face increasingly difficult choices in their serials acquisitions. As scholarly outputs continue to increase, and with the potentially dramatic impact of countries like China and India, this problem too can only get worse.

Copyright

> Nobody is making money with free content on the web, except search.
> People are used to reading everything on the net for free and that's going
> to have to change. (Rupert Murdoch, 'The Cable Show 09')

The whole web is going to have to confront a huge problem, namely, that
many of its users assume that everything they find on it should be free.
This is, of course, already an issue for the music industry, where illegal
peer-to-peer file sharing has decimated music sales; ever-increasing
bandwidth and the emergence of 'bit torrent' is having a similar impact
of the film industry, at least as far as the sales of DVDs go.

Indeed, online piracy is becoming an issue of concern for scholarly
publishers too. In addition to scholarly books and journal articles
appearing on general peer-to-peer file-sharing sites, a number of
websites dedicated to piracy of scholarly content have emerged.
Typically, these websites flagrantly violate international copyright law,
and even if the websites act on notices to take infringing material down
(as per the US Digital Millennium Copyright Act, DMCA), the
overhead for copyright owners in serving notices to remove material,
and more so in detecting the infringement in the first place, is
considerable. If piracy of scholarly material continues to grow it may
threaten the sustainability of current business models or force a move to
a model that makes content freely available on the open web, thus
eliminating the demand for pirated content. At least for some areas of
scholarly journal publishing there is an alternative, in the form of pay-
to-publish models. Scholarly books, like the music and film industry,
appear to have no such alternative on the horizon.

Intellectual property and the web

Far too often, copyright is incorrectly and unfairly painted as a barrier
to creativity, which stops users from doing what they want with
content. In fact, copyright law strikes a balance between making
material available for the good of the general public (via well defined
copyright exceptions) and providing a mechanism for remunerating
rights holders. Copyright is therefore an enabler, allowing creators and
rights holders to get fair reward for their intellectual property, and

providing an incentive for creativity and innovation.

There is a complicating factor in that there are differing policies from publisher to publisher, and even from journal to journal within the same publisher, with respect to the rights associated with particular pieces of work and what the authors and other users can and cannot do with different versions of an article. A study for the Publishing Research Consortium found that authors greatly underestimate what they can do with pre-publication versions of their articles but overestimate what they can do with the Version of Record (Morris, 2009). Standardization is difficult, due to the differing requirements of publishers and, more importantly, the needs of authors, which vary greatly from discipline to discipline.

However, far from being disassembled in our digital future, copyright will continue to have an extremely important role to play, but it does need to be constantly updated and supported by better technology that makes it easier for users to know what they can do with content that they find online. Clarity regarding the rights associated with a piece of work is in everyone's interests in order to maximize the opportunities afforded by the digital environment, and here initiatives like ACAP (the Automated Content Access Protocol) and ONIX-PL (ONline Information eXchange for Publications Licenses), which allow for the digital expression of rights, will be important enabling technologies, as metadata containing a machine-readable expression of rights are a requirement.[8]

Business models

Whether by subscriptions, author-side article charges, micropayments, blanket licence fees, advertising revenue, charitable donation, collective licensing or some new business model as yet unthought of, someone has to pay for the stewardship of digital material and professional, high-quality output. Otherwise, we face a chaotic web where we cannot tell what is worth reading and what can safely be ignored.

What's the Big Deal?

The online availability of journals has already allowed publishers to experiment with new business models. It is well known that, thanks to the marginal cost of making additional titles available online to subscribers, publishers with multiple titles have been able to offer 'big deals' – discounted bundles of journal titles – which have greatly increased the availability of journals at modest additional cost to the purchaser. Publishers of all sizes have also been able to sell to consortia of libraries or even to agree national site licence deals, such as via NESLi and NESLi2 in the UK and National Science and Technology Library (NSTL) in China, for electronic access.

Access for the developing world

In addition, the cost structures of the current system mean that publishers have been able to offer electronic journals to the developing world for free or at a greatly reduced price via programmes like HINARI (Health Inter Network Access to Research Initiative),[9] OARE (Online Access to Research in the Environment),[10] AGORA (Access to Global Online Research in Agriculture)[11] and PERii (Programme for the Enhancement of Research Information).[12] HINARI alone provides free access to 6200 leading biomedical and health journals and has 3500 registered institutions in 108 countries.

Any future changes to business models will have to ensure that the developing world can play a full part and this means that, as in the current system, those who can pay will have to subsidize those who cannot.

Open Access

Online availability of journals has also facilitated a multiplicity of free-to-read business models, known collectively as Open Access (OA). While the increased access and improved researcher efficiency brought about by changes to the established subscription model have gone largely unheralded, the same cannot be said of OA.

Established journal publishers have often been cast in the role of the pantomime villain in the OA debate. It is, though, untrue to say that publishers are anti-OA. A prominent feature in the mission statements and charters of almost all learned and professional societies is the promotion and dissemination of their subject, and in most cases this is the reason for their getting involved in publishing in the first place.

Commercial publishers, too, realize that widespread dissemination of the content that they publish is in everyone's interest. However, there has to be a viable and sustainable business model behind an industry that publishes 1.5 million research articles a year, and the debate within publishing houses revolves primarily around this rather than ideological arguments.

Two forms of OA seem to grab most of the headlines. In OA publishing (often referred to as the 'gold route') the final publisher version (the Version of Record) of the article is made freely available on the web immediately on publication. This is usually funded by author-side fees (for this reason often referred to as 'author pays', although in practice it is often a funding body or other organization that actually foots the bill), but a significant number of OA journals, more than half in the case of non-profit publishers (Cox and Cox, 2008), are funded by sponsorship, grants or subsidy from a parent institution or learned society. In manuscript archiving or self-archiving (known as the 'green route') authors deposit a version of their article in an open online repository. But there are two other forms of OA that receive less attention and yet are more widespread. In the delayed OA model the final, Version of Record articles appearing in subscription journals are made freely available after a certain period of time, while in the 'hybrid' model an author-side payment model runs alongside a subscription model so that authors can choose to make their articles immediately OA on payment of a fee or publish only to subscribers of the journal for free.

OA publishing (gold OA)

OA publishing is far from theoretical. Publishers are already operating the model based on subsidies or sponsorship, and there are successful 'author pays' journals and publishers operating in well funded areas like biomedicine (for example, journals from OA publishers Public Library of Science and BioMed Central, which is now part of Springer, and *Nucleic Acids Research* published by Oxford University Press), or where the publisher is able to take advantage of a low labour cost, for example the Egyptian-based Hindawi Publishing. Survey evidence shows that a quarter of publishers publish at least one fully OA journal (Cox and Cox, 2008), and this proportion is rising. Worryingly, though, other publishers have moved from a subscription publishing model to an 'author pays' model and back to a subscription model because they have been unable to sustain their operation on the basis of author pays (for example, *Journal of Clinical Investigation*).

OA publishing has advantages in that it provides a tangible revenue stream for publishers to pay for the cost of certification and dissemination, and it allows for the immediate dissemination of the Version of Record to anyone with an internet connection. However, there are concerns regarding the reliable and sustainable funding of author-side payment OA publishing, particularly in academic disciplines where research funding is relatively poor. The absolute, per article cost of publishing is likely to be broadly the same irrespective of discipline; current studies estimate this at around £3000 per paper (RIN, 2008; JISC, 2009). While this amounts to a modest and affordable 1–2% of research budgets in relatively well funded disciplines like biomedicine, it represents a much greater proportion of the research budget in disciplines like mathematics and ecology, where it will be more that 100% of current research budgets.

Clearly, if 'author pays' OA is to become the dominant economic model of scholarly publishing, then the funding mechanisms for the dissemination of research need to change dramatically. I hope that this becomes the case. Even so, author-side payment OA publishing is already mainstream and will continue to gain popularity in some disciplines.

Manuscript archiving (green OA)

Proponents of manuscript archiving (self-archiving or 'green' OA) see a mechanism by which authors can act to make all research immediately OA without either authors having to pay publication fees to journals or readers having to purchase access via a subscription. All that is required is online repositories – either institutionally based repositories or subject repositories – and the willingness of authors to deposit their manuscripts (see Ware (2004) for a discussion of the role of repositories).

Most publishers would agree that the outputs of publicly funded research should be freely available to the public, but would also point out that these 'outputs' are the Author Manuscript as submitted to the journal and before the publisher has added value in terms of quality assessment, association with the journal brand, addition of functionality like reference linking, and revision or correction in response to the peer-review or production processes.

Three issues need to be addressed if manuscript archiving is to be successful:

1 *Utilization by authors*
   The vast majority of journals allow their authors to do some form of self-archiving, on their own personal websites, in repositories run by their institution, in subject repositories for their discipline or a combination of these (Morris, 2009). Despite this, the take-up by authors has been low (Lawal, 2002; Rowlands and Nicholas, 2005; Davis and Connolly, 2007); voluntary manuscript archiving is estimated at 5–6% (Fowler, 2007). Several funding organizations[13] and research institutions have now introduced mandates requiring authors to deposit, which, combined with publishers depositing on behalf of authors, have improved deposit levels. The Wellcome Trust reports a compliance level of around 40% (Kiley, 2009), while for the National Institutes of Health compliance has increased from around 5% to circa 70% since its mandate became compulsory. Nonetheless, levels of self-archiving generally remain low.

2 *Reliance on journals for authority and certification*
   Material posted in online repositories currently relies on journal title or publisher brands for authority and certification. The major concern for publishers operating a subscription model is that widespread self-archiving will cause libraries to cancel their subscriptions. Despite anecdotal survey evidence (Ware, 2006), there is no empirical evidence attributing widespread subscription cancellations to manuscript archiving. The jury is still out, but it seems inconceivable that libraries will continue to subscribe to content that is also freely available on the web, so long as there is a high degree of confidence that it will continue to be available into the future. With budgets under constant pressure, what responsible librarian would? Of course, if self-archiving is complementary to subscription journals, then it comes at an additional cost in terms of the architecture and infrastructure of the repositories, in the cost of curation and preservation, and in the time of academics for archiving.

3 *Version control*

The third issue is a consequence of the first two. The version that publishers allow to be self-archived varies, and can be the Version of Record (though this is rare) or an earlier version of the article (Morris, 2009). Because the authority and certification of material appearing in online repositories is dependent on publisher brands, repositories therefore can and do contain a multiplicity of versions. Different versions of an article may appear in different repositories, with little or no version control and nothing to identify to the reader the way in which one version differs from another, with the obvious problems that this presents. As a result, some repositories insist that it is the Version of Record that is deposited, though this is the version that the journal is least likely to allow to be self-archived.

Hybrid model

The hybrid model allows journals funded by the tried and tested subscription model to experiment with OA in a low-risk way and to test their authors' appetite for author-side funded OA. It also allows subscription journals to comply with funder mandates requiring the final publisher version of articles to be made freely available on publication. The number of publishers offering a hybrid model more than tripled between 2005 and 2008 to 30% (Cox and Cox, 2008), but in some respects it is surprising that more publishers do not offer this option. This may be explained by the fact that OA has been less widely discussed in the arts and humanities than it has in science publishing, and that in any case take-up from authors has generally been low. The same survey reports that 53% of publishers offering a hybrid model have seen a take-up rate of 1% or less, 74% a take-up rate of 5% or less, rising to 91% of publishers seeing a take-up rate by authors of 10% or less.

Advertising

Advertising appears to be the business model of choice for the web. After all, it is how Google manages to generate revenues of $10 billion a year with a workforce of only 22,000 – not bad. And if it is good enough for Google, it should be good enough for the rest of us – right? I have lost count of the number of web businesses that had advertising as their core (and often only) revenue stream. Countless more have suggested advertising as the saviour for scholarly publishing.

Unfortunately advertising cannot be the business model that funds everything on the web – there are never going to be enough advertising dollars to go around. Scholarly material is characterized by high-value content, but with relatively few eyeballs looking at it, and is thus unattractive to potential advertisers. Indeed, if the web has taught us anything, it is that you need to be at a node of quite enormous traffic in order to make advertising a viable business model on a large scale, and currently that is the preserve of those offering search – and very few other businesses.

Future scenarios

If some form of OA is to become the dominant model of scholarly publishing, then there are four possible scenarios.

Scenario 1: subsistence

In this scenario there is widespread manuscript archiving but journals and online repositories coexist peacefully. The certification function continues to come from journals and their established brands, even if registration and dissemination do not, with the cost being met primarily through subscription income generated from sales to libraries. Version-control issues regarding manuscripts found in online repositories would be likely, so tension would build between repositories wanting to archive the definitive version of the article and the sizeable number of journals that did not allow the archiving of the Version of Record, in order to protect their subscription income. As a result, the full benefits of OA would not be achieved. Costs would be greater than under the subscription model, as the cost of both purchasing subscriptions and manuscript archiving (the cost of running and maintaining online repositories and the time spent by authors self-archiving) would have to be met. In addition, both journals and repositories would take on responsibility for the curation and preservation of the material they stewarded, with obvious duplication of cost. As mentioned above, it seems unlikely that librarians would continue to subscribe to a journal if the Version of Record of every article it published was deposited in online repositories. For this reason the probability of this scenario emerging as a stable dominant model for the majority of the literature is low.

Probability of dominance: Low
Benefits of OA: Not fully achieved
Preservation: Journals and repositories
Costs: Higher than present
Result: Order

Scenario 2: subvention

In this scenario funding is made available for author-side payments and there is a managed transition to OA publishing, whether or not there is widespread adoption of manuscript archiving leading to subscription cancellations. Journals therefore switch from a subscription model to an OA publishing mode of operation. Since the author-side payment mechanism does not conflict with manuscript archiving, journals are therefore able to sustain their operation and continue to provide the certification function on the literature. Journals may be more likely to allow the archiving of the Version of Record, but then again, they may not, in order to ensure that they generate web traffic, should this be important (and it probably will be, for example, for brand reinforcement or marketing to potential authors). The system would save on subscription costs, but most if not all of this expenditure would be transferred to author-side fees. The system would also have to bear the costs of manuscript archiving. Preservation and curation costs would also be duplicated. In addition, each article would be likely to appear in multiple repositories (given that more and more articles have authors from more than one institution, and the probable outcome that authors would need to archive in both institutional and subject repositories). Overall system costs would therefore be higher than in the present system, but the benefits of OA would be fully achieved and they might outweigh the costs. As mentioned previously, journals funded by author-side payments already appear viable in some well-funded disciplines, but in other fields the costs of publication are likely to be a much greater proportion of overall research grants – perhaps more than 100% – and for this reason it is unlikely that this will be the dominant scenario for all disciplines of academic endeavour in the short to medium term.

A variation of this scenario, suggested by some commentators, is that journals would no longer fulfil the dissemination function at all, and all access to journal articles would be via repositories (which presumably would need to be fully interoperable). Journals would still provide certification through the combination of peer review and association with their brands. In this case the outcome would be the same, except that dissemination, preservation and curation costs would not be duplicated.

Probability of dominance: High for some subject disciplines, low for others
Benefits of OA: Fully achieved
Preservation: Journals and repositories
Costs: Possibly lower than in Scenario 1, but higher than at present, assuming
     author-side payments amount to roughly the same as subscription outlay and
     there is duplication of access provision and preservation by journals and
     through a repository infrastructure
Result: Order

Scenario 3: substitution

In this scenario widespread manuscript archiving leads over time to large-scale cancellation of subscriptions to journals. No funding is made available for author-side payments and so journals go out of business, and with them disappears the certification provided by the combination of peer review and journal brands. However, given that 'necessity is the mother of invention', a new mechanism of certification quickly emerges to substitute for that provided by journals. It is difficult to speculate what this mechanism might be. Jensen (2007) suggests that 'heavily computed reputation-and-authority metrics' will form part of what he terms 'authority 3.0', but the details of any replacement system are, of course, unknown. It is therefore impossible to guess how widespread a new system could become and what it might cost. However, the costs of preservation and curation would fall only on the repository, so there would be at least a potential for the costs to be lower than in the current system, though once again each article would be likely to appear in multiple repositories. This scenario would offer the potential for the benefits of OA to be fully realized and, because a suitable alternative for the certification function had emerged, the scenario would result in order.

Probability of dominance: Medium
Benefits of OA: Fully achieved
Preservation: Repositories
Cost: Potentially lower than present
Result: Order

Scenario 4: subversion

In Scenario 4 widespread manuscript archiving leads over time to large-scale cancellation of subscriptions to journals. As in Scenario 3, no funding is made available for author-side payments and so journals go out of business and the certification provided by the combination of peer review and journal brands is lost. In this scenario no new suitable mechanism of certification emerges. Although the benefits of OA are realized, at least in theory, the lack of certification in the corpus of scholarly literature becomes an increasing problem, with readers having to spend more time evaluating what they find online. This problem is exacerbated for non-expert readers (lay consumers or those new to the field), who, without the benefit of established brands, find it even more difficult to ascertain what is trustworthy. The result is a chaotic environment for scholarly communication, and, while in theory the benefits of OA would be achieved, in practice the lack of trustworthiness of the literature would nullify any benefit. Similarly, while direct costs in the system might be reduced, each article would once again be likely to appear in multiple repositories. More consequentially, the increased time required to read and evaluate the literature would cause a drop in researcher productivity and a resultant increase in costs overall, given that the cost of search and reading is almost eight times that of publishing and distribution (RIN, 2008).

Probability of dominance: Medium
Benefits of OA: Not achieved?
Preservation: Repositories
Cost: Higher than present?
Result: Chaos

In practice, it is unlikely that any one of these scenarios would be played out in isolation. It is actually much more probable that they would all have a part to play to a greater or lesser extent, and that some would be more likely than others for certain disciplines of academic endeavour.

Conclusions

In periods of rapid change a little disorganization is inevitable. As in any process of evolution, blind alleys will be followed and there will be duplication of effort and expense. The aim, as the scholarly communication system evolves, is to ensure that there are no discontinuities of any of the important functional parts of the process, that one mechanism does not become extinct before another is mature enough to replace it.

There is much to do and there are challenging questions to be answered about who does it and how it is paid for. There are important and expensive issues of stewardship, particularly around version control, authority, the preservation and curation of digital material, research data and standards. Paying for this will also be challenging and all stakeholders in the scholarly communication chain will have to focus on efficiency and be ruthless regarding costs. A rapid move to an electronic-only environment would seem to be the most obvious initial priority and would be an avenue to substantial, achievable savings. As such, this should be pursued aggressively by all actors.

However the future detail of scholarly communication works out, the roles of publishers and librarians will become more, not less important. With a morass of information before them, readers will – more than ever before – need mechanisms, techniques, technology and, I am sure, trusted brands to help them sift the wheat from the chaff and find trustworthy, reliable content. That is not to say that what librarians and publishers do will remain the same. In fact, publishers and librarians will need to continue to change, and perhaps this transition will transform them almost beyond recognition. For publishers, there will continue to be both mixed business models and a mix of business models, and the world, as ever, will get more complex.

We will see new types of publisher and new types of librarian, but the role of librarians and publishers is to serve readers, and I am optimistic about the future of both.

Notes

1 www.isiwebofknowledge.com.
2 www.delicious.com.
3 www.citeulike.org.
4 www.connotea.org.
5 www.diigo.com.
6 www.portico.org; Lots of Copies Keep Stuff Safe, wwwlockss.org; www.kb.nl/hrd/dd/index-en.html.
7 www.crossref.org.
8 www.acap.org; www.editeur.org/21/ONIX-PL.
9 www.who.int/hinari/en.
10 www.oaresciences.org/en.
11 www.aginternetwork.org/en.
12 www.inasp.info/file/5f65fc9017860338882881402dc594e4/peri.html.
13 See www.sherpa.ac.uk/juliet/index.php.

References

Cox, J. and Cox, L. (2005) *Scholarly Publishing Practice Second Survey*, Association of Learned and Professional Society Publishers, www.alpsp.org/ngen_public/article.asp?id=200&did=47&aid=269&st=&oaid =-1 [accessed 22 July 2009].

Cox, J. and Cox, L. (2008) *Scholarly Publishing Practice Third Survey*, Association of Learned and Professional Society Publishers, www.alpsp.org/ngen_public/article.asp?id=200&did=47&aid=24781&st=&o aid=-1 [accessed 22 July 2009].

Crow, R. (2006) Publishing Cooperatives: an alternative for non-profit publishers, *First Monday*, 11 (9), http://firstmonday.org/htbin/cgiwrap/bin/ojs/index.php/fm/article/view/1396/ 1314 [accessed 17 July 2009].

Davis, P. M. and Connolly, M. J. L. (2007) Institutional Repositories: evaluating the reasons for non-use of Cornell University's installation of DSpace, *D-Lib Magazine*, 13 (3/4), www.dlib.org/dlib/march07/davis/03davis.html#12 [accessed 22 July 2009].

Digital Curation Centre (undated), www.dcc.ac.uk/about/what [accessed 19 April 2009].

Faraday, M. (1826) quoted in J. G. Crowther, *British Scientists of the Nineteenth Century*, Routledge and Kegan Paul Ltd, 1935, 96.

Fowler, N. (2007) *Scientific Publication: trends, challenges, opportunities*, EU Conference on Scientific Publishing, Brussels, 15 February, http://ec.europa.eu/research/science-society/document_library/pdf_06/ fowler-022007_en.pdf [accessed 22 July 2009].

Jensen, M. (2007) The New Metrics of Scholarly Authority, *Chronicle of Higher Education*, 15 June, http://chronicle.com/article/The-New-Metrics-of-scholarly/5449 [accessed 4 November 2009].

JISC (2009) *Economic Implications of Alternative Scholarly Publishing Models*, http://jisc.ac.uk/media/documents/publications/rpteconomicoapublishing.pdf [accessed 22 July 2009].

Kiley, R. (2009) Open Access Mandates: view from the Wellcome Trust, *Research in the Open: how mandates work in practice, RSP/RIN Conference*, www.rsp.ac.uk/events/MandatesDay2009/oa_mandates_may_2009.ppt [accessed 22 July 2009].

Krane, B. (2006) *Researchers Find Kids Need Better Online Academic Skills*, http://advance.uconn.edu/2006/061113/06111308.htm [accessed 7 July 2009].

Lawal, I. (2002) Scholarly Communication: the use and non-use of e-print archives for the dissemination of scientific information, *Issues in Science and Technology Librarianship*, Fall, www.istl.org/02-fall/article3.html [accessed 22 July 2009].

Mabe, M. (2003) The Growth and Number of Journals, *Serials*, 16 (2), 191–7, http://uksg.metapress.com/media/3appuvttvjrb76qugt33/contributions/f/1/9/5/ f195g8ak0eu21muh.pdf.

Mabe, M. and Amin, M. (2001) Growth Dynamics of Scholarly and Scientific Journals, *Scientometrics*, 51 (1), 147–62, www.springerlink.com/content/x235508307.

Morris, S. (2009) *Journal Authors' Rights: perception and reality*, Publishing Research Consortium, www.publishingresearch.org.uk/documents/JournalAuthorsRights.pdf [accessed 19 June 2009].

NISO (2008) *NISO RP-8-2008, Journal Article Versions (JAV): recommendations of the NISO/ALPSP JAV Technical Working Group*, www.niso.org/publications/rp [accessed 17 July 2009].

RIN (Research Information Network) (2008) *Activities, Costs and Funding Flows in the Scholarly Communications System in the UK*, www.rin.ac.uk/files/Income-&-cost-flows-report-(full-version)-final.pdf [accessed 22 July 2009].

Roosendaal, H. E. and Geurts, P. A. T. M. (1997) Forces and Functions in Scientific Communication: an analysis of their interplay. In Karttunen, M., Holmlund, K. and Hilf, E. R. (eds), *Cooperative Research Information Systems in Physics*, Oldenburg University, http://doc.utwente.nl/60395/1/Roosendaal97forces.pdf [accessed 22 July 2009].

Rowlands, I. and Nicholas, D. (2005) *New Journal Publishing Models: an international survey of senior researchers*, www.ucl.ac.uk/ciber/ciber_2005_survey_final.pdf [accessed 22 July 2009].

Russell, I. (2009) *ALPSP Survey of Librarians: responding to the credit crunch – what now for librarians and libraries?*, www.alpsp.org/ngen_public/article.asp?aID=112716 [accessed 4 November 2009].

Shotton, D. (2009) Semantic Publishing: the coming revolution in scientific journal publishing, *Learned Publishing*, 22 (2), 85–94.

Shotton, D., Portwin, K., Klyne, G. and Miles, A. (2009) Adventures in Semantic Publishing, *PLoS Computational Biology*, 5 (4), www.ploscompbiol.org/article/info%3Adoi%2F10.1371%2Fjournal.pcbi.1000361 [accessed 22 July 2009].

Thurman, N. and Myllylahti, M. (2009) Taking the Paper out of News: a case study of Taloussanomat, Europe's first online-only newspaper, *Journalism Studies*, 10 (5), http://works.bepress.com/cgi/viewcontent.cgi?article=1005&context= neil_thurman [accessed 22 July 2009].

Van de Sompel, H., Payett, S., Erickson, J., Lagoze, C. and Warner, S. (2004) Rethinking Scholarly Communication, *D-Lib Magazine*, 10 (9), www.dlib.org/dlib/september04/vandesompel/09vandesompel.html [accessed 17 July 2009].

Velterop, J. (1995) Keeping the Minutes of Science. In *Proceedings of Electronic Libraries and Visual Information Research (ELVIRA) Conference*, Aslib, London, May 2–4, organized by De Montfort University (eds), Milton Keynes.

Wang, Ying (2007) How Learning Chinese Has Been Made Easy, *China Daily*, 25 July.

Ware, M. (2004) Institutional Repositories and Scholarly Publishing, *Learned Publishing*, 17 (2), 115–24.

Ware, M. (2006) *ALPSP Survey of Librarians on Factors in Journal Cancellation*, Association of Learned and Professional Society Publishers, www.alpsp.org/ngen_public/article.asp?id=200&did=47&aid=157&st=&oaid =-1 [accessed 22 July 2009].

Wells, W. A. (2007) The Returning Tide: how China, the world's most populous country, is building a competitive research base, *Journal of Cell Biology*, 178 (4), 376–401.

4

E-books and scholarly communication futures

Colin Steele

Given the absolute faculty of reading, the task of going through the
pages of a book must be, of all tasks, the most certainly within the grasp
of the man or woman who attempts it! Alas, no; – if the habit be not
there, of all tasks it is the most difficult. If a man have not acquired the
habit of reading till he be old, he shall sooner in his old age learn to
make shoes than learn the adequate use of a book. And worse again; –
under such circumstances the making of shoes shall be more pleasant to
him than the reading of a book. Let those who are not old, – who are
still young, ponder this well.   (Trollope, 1866)

Introduction: the impact of the digital revolution

It is a truth universally acknowledged that in the 21st century we are
witnessing a revolution in communication unparalleled since the
invention of the printing press in the 15th century. As in the 15th
century, however, there is a time lag between technical innovation and
the impact on society of changes in the distribution and publishing of
scholarly knowledge. Initially, the first printed pages of incunabula
replicated the physical layout of manuscripts, and in the same way
digital journals and books have remained influenced by historical print
and research assessment frameworks.

In the monastic scriptorium, the dissemination of knowledge was
limited by the productivity of the output of the scribes and by public
accessibility to appropriate libraries or personal collections. Books

generally impacted little on the general public, for whom oral transmission (perhaps now called social networking) was the norm for conveying knowledge and gossip. With the introduction of movable type, these access limitations were overcome quantitatively, although it was probably not until the second half of the 19th century that the mass of the reading public and the print world significantly coincided. By the 19th century, books were no longer individually crafted works of art, but products of industry in a variety of formats (Battles, 2009).

E-books, by which one means the text rather than the device, are another significant variant in the evolution of book publishing and distribution. As Siracusa (2009) contends, an issue 'is right there in the name: e-*book*. In the print world, the word "book" is used to refer to both the content and the medium. In the digital realm, "e-book" refers to the content only – or rather, that's the intention. Unfortunately, the conflation of these two concepts in the nomenclature of print naturally carries over to the digital terminology, much to the confusion of all.' For the purpose of this chapter, e-book means 'born digital'.

In one sense, it could be said the historical print world focused on a process in which the final product went through a series of sequential stages to reach the final text. Now the immediacy of the internet provides a myriad of different knowledge distribution paths. We are moving from a world of review then publish, to publish then review for many outside controlled, scholarly environments.

However, if one were now able to establish *de novo* the production and distribution of academic knowledge in the digital era, it is unlikely that the present publishing formats would result. Not only have the internet and the rise of associated outlets broadened the geographic scope of scholarly communication beyond that of the print environment, but new mechanisms of social dialogue, such as blogs and Open Access (OA) frameworks, have emerged.

Reading the change?

New methods of textual output and sharing have an impact on modes of transmission and attention. Social networking tools such as Twitter, Blogger, Facebook and YouTube are allegedly impacting on attention spans, particularly of Generation Y, and resulting in lack of appreciation of book formats and lengthy texts. Jeff Bezos, Amazon's CEO, has stated that 'long-form reading is losing ground to short-form reading . . . we change our tools and our tools change us' (Feldman, 2009). Power browsing is the norm for the internet's 'promiscuous users', who want instant online access, preferably for free.

Rosen (2008) worries that 'collaborative "information foraging" will replace solitary deep reading; the connected screen will replace the disconnected book . . . Literacy, the most empowering achievement of our civilization, is to be replaced by a vague and ill-defined screen savvy. The paper book, the tool that built modernity, is to be phased out in favor of fractured, unfixed information. All in the name of progress.' But then, in 1477 the Venetian humanist Hieronimo Squarciafico worried that an abundance of books would lead to intellectual laziness, making men 'less studious'. *Plus ça change.*

Noted science fiction author and physics professor Gregory Benford (2009) reflects that 'people read like crazy on the Internet – but they are not reading 60,000 narratively coherent words in a row ... they live within a flow of mediated micro particles'. Carr (2008) believes that he can no longer connect with long articles or books the way he used to: 'And what the Net seems to be doing is chipping away my capacity for concentration and contemplation. My mind now expects to take in information the way the Net distributes it: in a swiftly moving stream of particles. Once I was a scuba diver in the sea of words. Now I zip along the surface like a guy on a Jet Ski.'

Rosen (2008) quotes the noted critic George Steiner from a 1988 *Times Literary Supplement* article: 'I would not be surprised if that which lies ahead for classical modes of reading resembles the monasticism from which those modes sprung. I sometimes dream of *houses of reading* – a Hebrew phrase – in which those passionate to learn to read well would find the necessary guidance, silence and complicity of disciplined companionship.' Words reflected by Terry Pratchett, the English author, when I interviewed him in 2007. He decried the transformation of the English public library into a noisy internet café-cum-mall, favouring a return to quiet places in public libraries. Maybe the wheel will turn and libraries will provide monastic e-cubicles of silence amid the noise of the information commons and the decline in public space etiquette.

Similar trends in changes in reading patterns and attention spans have been reflected in analyses of usage of the scientific literature. The time available to scientists to read articles has declined almost in proportion to the growth of scientific literature itself. Coates (2009) has reflected on a knowledge overload: 'and so, we read indexes rather than journals, abstracts rather than papers, review essays rather than books. Awash in a sea of academic discourse and analysis, we look desperately for an intellectual life-raft, all the while feverishly seeking to add to the accumulated scholarly wisdom ourselves.'

Unfortunately the deluge of publications from the academic community is set to increase as university administrators and funding authorities place an arguably wrong emphasis on the value of publication metrics and journal rankings to establish research-quality frameworks, and thus funding. These metrics, however, can be manipulated and lead to significant unforeseen changes in academic scholarly communication and publishing practices, which is often not anticipated by those who change the ground rules (Steele, Butler and Kingsley, 2006).

Changes in publishing settings

The changes in economic settings from late 2008 onwards have raised questions as to appropriate global models for the 21st century in areas ranging from banking to the car industry. The anticipated demise of the printed newspaper has occupied many column inches, both online and in print, and now the same angst is prevailing in the publishing industry (Engelhardt, 2008). Robinson (2009) has argued that 'this is not to say that the book is doomed. But publishers will surely have to change the way they do business. . . . An industry that spends all its money on bookseller discounts and very little on finding an audience is getting things the wrong way round.' Most academic books, under current models, have limited print runs, sales and, thus, audiences.

The first years of the 21st century have seen a very significant development in open access to information. How this will play out in the coming years in terms of the economics of scholarship and scholarly communication will be an intriguing process. There may well be a transformation in the traditional flows and costs of scholarly publishing to rectify the situation whereby universities give away most of their research and provide mostly free peer-review services towards the finished product, which university libraries then buy back. The increasing adoption of Open Access (OA) mandates by the UK Research Councils to ensure 'public funding, public access, public good' will undoubtedly continue. We can only distribute and access effectively what we own.

Universities are also recognizing the need for change in access for a variety of reasons. The economic downturn has impacted severely on library budgets, particularly, for the first time in decades, in the USA. The research community there has been largely protected until now by the strength of its libraries, but with 50% of Harvard's library acquisition budget being funded from endowment returns, even the world's richest university is feeling the pain. Is it any coincidence that Harvard's OA policy emerged in 2008, attempting to protect the copyright of its research output and to ensure its effective distribution on a global scale?

Massachusetts Institute of Technology (MIT) announced in March 2009 that it will make its research available to the public free of charge, becoming the first US university to mandate the policy across all departments. MIT's policy is based on that adopted by Harvard's Faculty of Arts and Sciences in 2008, and retains non-exclusive publication rights for its authors to advance research and education by making them globally available (Lauerman, 2009). Academic e-monographs can readily be accommodated in such frameworks.

At the time of writing, in mid 2009, a number of the major commercial US publishing houses are experiencing significant downturns in their operations, as indeed are major bookseller chains such as Borders and Barnes & Noble. The editor of *Publishers Weekly* (before she left the company in late January 2009) was quoted as saying that 2009 would be 'the worst year for publishing in decades'. Many commercial publishers have thus decided to utilize new social media in order to promote their publications. Ettinghausen (2008) reported that Penguin at that time had:

> 5,000 friends on Facebook, we're on Twitter, and were the first to go into Second Life, where we took William Gibson, the writer who invented the word cyberspace. We don't believe books will disappear – 99 per cent of our revenue still comes from ink on paper – but the way people read will change. People have shorter attention spans – a website has about three seconds to capture their attention. As a result we are spending time learning from what Nike, Sony, Xbox, YouTube do – we're competing for people's entertainment time, particularly with a young audience.

Self-publishing and widespread access to publications is encapsulated by Scribd (www.scribd.com/about), 'the place where you publish, discover and discuss original writings and documents'. 'YouTube for documents' is the term used to describe Scribd, with more than 50,000 new documents being posted daily at the time of writing (Flood, 2009). If new modes of publishing take off, then the opportunities for authors, through wider web distribution, could lead to significant shifts in the marketing of and access to book content. A relevant point in this context is that most authors, despite being the content creators, receive relatively little financial reward for their books, as well as limited print life. If digital distribution and preservation patterns change, then the author's lot can be improved in terms of both remuneration and access.

And whither unpublished academic research? Alexander (2009) claims that 'keeping in mind that university presses publish roughly 10,000 new books annually, and assuming that they publish only 1 out of every 10 manuscripts, that means university presses are filtering 100,000 manuscripts per year. Of those, probably 15,000–20,000 get sent out for peer review.' There is a huge amount of unproductive academic time going into publishing processes, with limited outcomes. Would it be better to re-engineer resources in the press context, perhaps to establish a Scribd-type environment for academia via cross-searchable institutional repositories?

Digital POD futures

While most books are created and published digitally, distribution patterns reflect the pre-internet era. Even if the text is transmitted digitally across continents, as is the case with many fiction books in Australia, physical books are still then shipped to customers via bookshops from publishers' warehouses. On average, books remain for shorter periods in bookshops, where it is not unknown for publishers to pay for premium space at the front of the shop. Books unsold are returned and subsequently either remaindered or pulped. So in effect the customer is paying for both the creation and the destruction of a book. This is an increasingly uneconomic and inefficient distribution and stock control process, which will eventually be overtaken by digital delivery directly to bookshops and libraries within e-preservation frameworks and print-on-demand (POD) options.

Jason Epstein, the former editorial director at Random House, promulgated POD delivery in *The Book Business* (2001). Epstein's vision is now becoming a reality as the Espresso Book Machine (EBM) is being introduced into bookshops in a number of countries. The major British bookseller chain of Blackwell introduced its first EBM into one of its London stores in April 2009. The University of Michigan Library has installed an EBM, which can produce a paperback book on demand in about five minutes at roughly $10 per book. These are usually reprints of public domain titles from the library's digitized collection of nearly two million books, as well as books available from the Open Content Alliance.

Cox (2008) aptly notes that with the POD, the 'future of the printed monograph has arrived'. Cox outlines the benefits of the EBM, particularly in the delivery of text across distances, citing the collaboration between OECD Publishing and DA Information Services in Melbourne. Cox sees not only speed of delivery, but also a contribution to global greening. The OECD (Organisation for Economic Cooperation and Development) believes that such a process to Australia will save over 12 lbs or 5.8 kg in carbon emissions per book sold. Surface mail to Australia currently takes three months from Europe, whereas a text can be delivered on site in three minutes. The issues for libraries and their technical processing are also relevant here in terms of future ordering, receipt and distribution patterns. Once the price of EBMs reduces, there is no doubt there will be a much more rapid take-up in bookshops and libraries.

Willes, in *Reading Matters* (2008), reminds us, however, that nothing really changes in conceptual terms of production, only the technology. In her book she features a photograph of the famous British publisher Allen Lane with his 1930s 'Penguincubator', a slot machine which dispensed Penguin paperbacks at sixpence a time directly to the reader. This was undoubtedly a precursor to the public EBM.

Who owns information in the digital era?

In historical terms, whoever dominated the trade routes dominated the world, as exemplified by the Dutch, French and British empires. The control of natural resources, such as oil and gas, has been another major factor in power structures to the present day. Who now controls and owns information has been an emerging debate since the 1950s, as the science, technical and medical (STM) publishing world has been dominated by a relatively small number of large multinational publishers, to the detriment of the output of smaller publishers, learned societies and book purchasing by university libraries.

Firms that begin small and emerge as giants en route often lose their pioneering zeal to the god of Mammon – think Microsoft and Reed Elsevier. It could be argued that Amazon and Google are moving down that track. Google's digitization programme currently adds another layer to the complexities of the publishing world. The US Google Book Search settlement has produced both positive and negative feedback.

The Google debate

A key player in the Google debate to date has been Professor Robert Darnton, Director of Harvard University Library. Darnton (2009) is concerned that 'Google will enjoy what can only be called a monopoly . . . of access to information . . . what worries me is the fact that Google has no competitors. The downside has to do with the danger of monopoly.' Darnton feels that we now 'have a situation where Google can really ratchet up prices, and that's what really worries me . . . There's no real authority to enforce fair pricing . . . I'm worried that Google will be the Elsevier of the future, but magnified by a hundred times' (Oder, 2009).

In a forum at Columbia University on 13 March 2009, Alexander Macgillivray, then Associate General Counsel for Products and Intellectual Property at Google, and now General Counsel at Twitter, responded to these issues by 'reading the pricing objectives in the settlement: the realization of revenue at market rates and the realization of broad access to books by the public'. He suggested that 'there's an enforceable provision that limits pricing' (Oder, 2009). The debate continues at the time of writing (Summer 2009), but very important long-term issues are at stake here. The fact that Google is offering to make texts available in the USA via a single free-access terminal in every public library building means that public access to content will be available in a way not previously possible; but it does place a very restricted view on access – to one terminal in one physical location – which runs contrary to the patterns of 'access anywhere, anytime' of Generation Y.

Google's restrictions on textual access outside of the USA – because of copyright caution about territorial rights – is an example of digital narrowness. This blockage of access to users outside the USA will fall within the framework of the 'tragedy of the anti-commons': 'Will it matter that Google Book Search, when it is marketed as a commercial subscription service for libraries and universities, cannot be accessed or read in the world at large? ... Yes, it will matter, and that it matters will be another instance of the tragedy of the anti-commons' (Hodgkin, 2009).

Brewster Kahle, who has laboured long for free access to digital information through his Internet Archive, has noted that Google restricts scanned books to Google search only and enforces restrictions on some uses of public domain books, even those scanned from public institutions, like the University of Michigan, with whom it co-operates:

Although the library [Michigan] can share content with other libraries, it cannot provide the optical character recognition (OCR) of the books to individuals, even if the content is in the public domain. If the texts had been self-scanned, some of the limitations would not be in place, and the library would be freer to share its content. . . . Libraries will be able to sign up for a subscription to view copyrighted material that has been digitized by Google partners, but a subscription won't be needed to access public domain materials. . . . Although there are indications that subscriptions will be reasonably priced, some have been wary of the agreement with Google, noting that there is no guarantee that the costs for subscriptions would be or stay low. The outcome of negotiations around subscription prices for Google partners and others is yet to be determined. (Guevara, 2009)

Synergies for the library, institutional academic publishing and the campus bookstore

When I gave the Follett Lectures in Britain in 1995, Google was not even on the horizon. In those lectures I stated:

In this process of integration of services, the publishing activities on campus must not be forgotten. The Campus Bookshop, the printing and multimedia services, the network backbone providers will need to come together with libraries to provide a structured network integration of services. It may well be that campus bookshops as we know them will disappear in a networked environment as will certain of the book supplier middlemen unless they restructure. University presses, a declining force in recent years, may well become transformed as they mutate into distributors of information from their own and other universities in electronic format, thereby making available information that was too prohibitively expensive to produce and distribute in conventional form. (Steele, 1995)

A decade later, the integration of POD production, publishing and libraries is becoming increasingly feasible, as developments at Sydney and Michigan universities have confirmed. As students reduce their purchasing of books and textbooks, the offerings of the campus bookstore have largely become a mixture of university memorabilia, paperbacks and course reading material. Meanwhile, university libraries are moving large numbers of books and bound serials into off-campus stores so that information/learning commons facilities can be installed. The similarities in access to and provision of information 'fast food' will blur and integrate the roles of the library and campus bookstore.

The historic decline of the academic monograph

Bauerlein (2009), citing Association of Research Libraries data, reveals that the number of monographs purchased by US research libraries rose just 1% between 1986 and 2006. The British Academy (2005) was greatly concerned about the impact of such trends and the decline of the scholarly monograph:

In the 1960s and 1970s, far fewer monographs were published than now, with routine global sales of 1500 or more. But these sales levels were not sustained, and a declining sales step-curve has been evident throughout the past quarter century, with a vicious circle of declining sales driving higher prices driving declining sales. Individual publishers have responded by issuing more and more individual titles, but with lower expectations of each. Global sales can now be as low as 250 or 300 in some fields. At some point in the 1990s, the UK academy ceased to be a self-sustaining monographic community: the subjects that have survived and/or thrived in this context have been those (like economics or linguistics or classics) with international appeal.

In the increasingly complex world of digital scholarship the individual researcher is often out of touch, for a variety of reasons, with the problems and solutions to scholarly communication issues. Thompson (2005) argued that while many academics 'depend on the presses to publish their work . . . they generally know precious little about the forces driving presses to act in ways that are sometimes at odds with the aims and priorities of academics . . . the monograph can survive only if the academic community actively support it'.

Whither the university press?

Historically, university presses were established to distribute the scholarship of their university (Steele, 2008). They lost their way, in this context, in the last decades of the 20th century, when commercial publishers, mostly in Europe, grew rapidly to fill the publishing vacuum in the post-Sputnik expansion funding of university research. The rise of the multinational STM 'Big Deals' and the decline in university library budgets in real terms saw a significant reduction by libraries in the purchasing of monographs and the output of learned societies and small publishers.

Big Deals can bring considerable benefits and underpin research by making a far greater range of material widely available at the desktop, so naturally they are very popular with researchers, who are, however, largely distanced from the issues of scholarly communication and the ever-increasing costs of subscriptions. The UK Research Information Network (2009) has outlined the advantages of Big Deals with university libraries, but has also cautioned that they 'bring risks: libraries are often locked for several years into deals that may take up 75% or more of their acquisition budgets, leaving them little scope to spend funds on other materials, particularly monographs'. Books are especially in danger in budget downturns because they are, in a sense, paid for out of disposable income in a way fixed serial subscriptions are not. So, just as casual staff are laid off before tenured staff in universities, books are simply not ordered, so as to meet budget shortfalls.

A decline in revenues led many university press publishers away from their academic core business to publishing products which were often indistinguishable from those of wholly commercial trade publishers. University presses found themselves in a quandary. On the one hand, they had a foundation brief to publish original and often esoteric scholarship, but on the other, they needed to achieve financial viability. They were between an academic publishing rock and a financial hard place.

Sutherland (2007) has also commented on the differing standards of university presses and their monographic output:

> There are, as every wide-awake academic knows, presses with acceptance hurdles so low that a scholarly mole could get over them. They edit minimally, publish no more than the predictable minimum library sale (200 or so) and make their money from volume. They repay their authors neither in money nor prestige. They put out a few good books; and a lot of the other kind. The best imprints (Oxford and Cambridge University Press, for example) set the bar deterringly high. A scholarly kangaroo will have trouble clearing their hurdle.   (Sutherland, 2007).

The £2 million losses of Cambridge University Press, however, as reported in April 2009, mean that one of these two publishing kangaroos has lost some of its publishing bounce. During 2008 and 2009 a number of smaller American university presses experienced significant financial downturns, the University of Missouri Press and the University of New Mexico Press, at the time of writing, being the latest examples. In these trends, the university press often has become disengaged from its parent institution. Within new frameworks of institutional scholarly communication, the digital era provides the opportunity for new models for the academic monograph.

New institutional scholarly frameworks

The Ithaka Report *University Publishing in a Digital Age* reaffirmed the relative isolation of many American university presses from their core administrative structures: 'Publishing generally receives little attention from senior leadership at universities, and the result has been a scholarly-publishing industry that many in the university community find to be increasingly out of step with the important values of the academy' (Brown, Griffiths and Rascoff, 2007). There are, however, increasing initiatives to reconnect the university press to the scholarly communication process within universities. Hahn (2008) noted in a survey of the 123 members of the Association of Research Libraries (ARL) that the majority were 'either producing publications or developing publishing services'.

The Association of American Universities (AAU), the ARL, the Coalition for Networked Information and the National Association of State Universities and Land-Grant Colleges issued a collective call for action in early 2009 that urged universities to become leaders in spreading research and scholarship (AAU et al., 2009): 'Digital technologies have opened the door to a host of new possibilities for sharing knowledge and generated entirely new forms of content that must be made broadly available. This shift demands that universities take on a much more active role in ensuring dissemination of the knowledge produced by their institutions – both now and in the future' (Lynch, 2009).

The main drawbacks in terms of immediate change are the conservative and rigid concepts of judging excellence for tenure and promotion that are embodied by the book. Another Ithaka report has highlighted the problems between the potential of new models of scholarly communication and the fact that 'anything that doesn't look like a traditional work of scholarship is not a scholarly work; thus the immutability of traditional publishing models becomes axiomatic' (Maron and Smith, 2008). The book is still seen as the metric par excellence for the humanities and parts of the social sciences in the international research assessment exercises.

We thus are confronted by a situation in which the mechanisms for the digital distribution of academic monograph are increasing, yet academic conservatism and research evaluation standards currently negate a variety of forms of e-production. E-books, in particular, have been viewed as less 'academic' than their print counterparts, yet they experience the same peer-review processes and can be available just as easily as print, through POD outlets.

A University College London (2009) survey on the role and future of the monograph in the arts and humanities notes, in the words of one interviewee, that 'monographs are like the main course of a meal, journal articles and other scholarly communication are like tapas and the monograph represents the "gold standard"'. The physical appearance of the monograph, however, is not enough to constitute the intellectual meal. Effective distribution of the content will ensure that all get their just desserts.

Another UCL interviewee felt that 'most people appear to rely on contacts or reconnections, such as one's PhD supervisor, to get published'. Kingsley (2009) has noted in her doctoral thesis, in which she interviewed academics at the Australian National University (ANU) and the University of New South Wales, that many researchers were unfamiliar with recent developments in digital scholarship and e-publishing, and that researchers often continued to reflect publishing frameworks from their own early research experiences, thereby giving advice to current doctoral students which was largely out of date.

A case study of the ANU E-Press

The potential for more effective distribution of university scholarship can be seen in the following example. Professor Oskar Spate's award-winning book *The Spanish Lake* (1979) was a critical and commercial success for the then ANU Press, but after it went out of print copies soon became difficult to find. By 2005 there were only two copies of *The Spanish Lake* listed on Antiquarian Book Exchange (ABE), both at prices over $400. Subsequently, the ANU E-Press published the book free online in 2004 and the Spanish government supported a Spanish translation, *El Lago Español*, in 2006, which saw just over 28,000 complete PDF downloads in 2008. There is surely no contest in the ability to distribute scholarship in the new e-press frameworks. The costs are relatively small in the totality of library or information budgets, let alone the university as a whole (Steele, 2008).

ANU E-Press titles are freely available in HTML, PDF and mobile device formats and are discoverable through Google Book Search and Google Scholar. A total of 8643 print-on-demand copies were sold between January and December 2008. Since the E-Press's monographs are downloadable free, around the world, high print sales were not the original aim, but clearly these are growing. Annual ANU E-Press statistics for PDF and HTML downloads for 2005–8 were:

2005	381,740
2006	745,288
2007	1,252,735
2008	2,747,445

Contrast these figures with the average print run of a monograph cited by the British Academy. The PDF top five global downloads in 2008 were as follows:

1	*El Lago Español*	46,394 (28,041 complete book)
2	*Ethics and Auditing*	46,310 (22,354 complete book)
3	*The Islamic Traditions of Cirebon*	41,532 (19,692 complete book)
4	*The Austronesians*	38,750 (24,839 complete book)
5	*Myanmar: the state, community and the environment*	34,876 (24,882 complete book)

Outside looking in or inside looking out?

One sometimes feels, however, that if it does not happen in the USA, it doesn't happen. Thus Antipodean e-presses were somewhat taken aback when various US educational outlets announced in March 2009 that University of Michigan Press (UM Press) was the first to move to a digital free, online monograph model with POD sales. This was some three to four years after the launch of Australian e-press initiatives with the same model (Steele, 2008). Michigan's provost stated that 'a university press should be judged by its contribution to scholarship and that university presses have been "marginalized" by their economic challenges' (Jaschik, 2009).

The UM Press release notes that 'digital publishing helps the UM Press to adopt a business model more consistent with the university research goal to disseminate information as widely and freely as possible' (University of Michigan, 2009). The digital model will allow 'enhanced digital options, including hot links, graphics, 3D animation and video'. Publishers have been changing content and formats to reflect economic circumstances. Even major publishers like Oxford University Press, however, are dropping or repositioning footnotes because of costs. Digital e-books with hyperlinks not only to footnotes but also to additional content, as at Michigan and Sydney university presses, are the means of overcoming the restrictions of print.

Crane (2009) and his colleagues have commented: 'we must now face the challenge of rebuilding our infrastructure in a digital form. Much of the intellectual capital that we accumulated in the twentieth century is inaccessible, either because its print format does not lend itself to conversion into a machine-actionable form or because commercial entities own the rights and the content is not available under the open-licensing regimes necessary for eScience in general and ePhilology in particular.' Lynch (2005) has noted:

> The problems are cultural, generational, and, to some extent, based on the unfamiliar nature of the digital genres. In the networked information environment, they now have a growing range of alternative genres through which to communicate and share their research. We may begin to see a significant sociological shift in the humanities and social sciences toward a more collaborative scholarship that embraces both individual analytical and critical work and the creation of large community knowledge bases. Balancing and integrating individual and community perspectives in these knowledge bases will be a fascinating and fertile process. . . . Over the next decade, our challenges will be twofold: We must find ways to formalize and underwrite these efforts on an institutional basis, recognizing that they will strengthen research, scholarship, teaching, and learning in all the disciplines, but particularly in the social sciences and humanities. And we must ensure that the new genres are institutionalized, managed, and preserved as effectively as is the traditional print monograph.

University scholarly one-stop shops?

The UM Press is being 'restructured as an academic unit under the Dean of Libraries, placing the publishing house at the centre of the University's digitization efforts' (Swanson, 2009). This process of scholarly communication integration on campus, however, should not be restricted to the university press. There is a growing tendency within universities to bring together their research outputs, making the publications of the university globally available in a one-stop shop repository. These outputs include opinion pieces, working papers, digital theses, pre- and post-prints and associated research data, and repositories are seen as making them more accessible and branding the university's output. The fact that the more formal peer-reviewed outputs of the university are required for research assessment exercises, notably in the UK, Australia and New Zealand, has led to the development and promotion of institutional repositories as the focal point of university research in a collective sense.

The collecting of publications for research assessment exercises such as the UK's Research Evaluation Framework (REF) and Australia's Excellence in Research Assessment (ERA) provides university platforms for the initial stocking of repositories. In this process, OA e-books can just as easily be collected and/or linked within the segments of the repository. As a by-product of these repository downloads, there is no reason why downloads and associated metrics should not be considered in assessment procedures.

California eScholarship is now one of the success stories in the distribution of institutional scholarship. This repository is part of the California Digital Library initiative. The research and scholarly output that it includes are selected and deposited by the individual University of California units. On 2 April 2009 the website recorded 35,042 full-text downloads of repository content in the previous week, while total full-text downloads to that date were 8,026,215.

Commercial publisher OA initiatives

It is relevant in this context that in late 2008 the major UK publisher Bloomsbury (publisher of the *Harry Potter* series) established an 'on-demand' imprint which would publish titles online for free (Pinter, 2008). Bloomsbury Academic will use Creative Commons licences to allow non-commercial use of all its titles online as soon as they are published, with revenue being generated from print copies sold using short-run technologies and POD. This is apparently the first time a commercial publisher has devoted a whole imprint to the model.

Pinter notes:

> It's a totally different paradigm. . . . If you start with the assumption that everything you access should be paid for at the point of use, then what we are doing is charity. If you take the view that the Internet should be more of a library and less of a bookstore, and that one way of funding the publishing process is through those who access books, then free [online] access is not charitable, it's just part of the way you do business. . . . I am going to have to sell enough copies of my books to keep my business alive. I expect to lose a few sales [because the material is available online

for free] but gain a few sales because more people will know about the work. If I'm right, we'll be profitable. If I'm wrong, I'll get kicked out.

(Pinter, 2008)

Bloomsbury Academic aims to publish 40 to 50 titles in its first year. The jury is still out, given that it is only early days, but this certainly throws down the gauntlet to many traditional university presses. Another interesting variant is Faber's 'pay-what-you-want ebook', giving readers the chance to pay what they believe is appropriate for historian Ben Wilson's latest book, *What Price Liberty?* Its print price is £14.99, with Faber giving readers the opportunity to set their own price, or even download for free. Faber is expecting the experiment to increase the sales of the printed book, 'adding sales rather than replacing them' (Lea 2009). A number of internet commentators, such as Doctorow (2007), have argued that putting your material free online leads to more print sales, through either traditional publishers or POD outlets.

The Open Monograph Press (OMP) software will also encourage an alternative approach to monograph publishing. OMP is 'based on a modular design for an online system that would foster, manage, and publish monographs in digital and print forms using open-source software developments, drawn from journal publishing, and social networking technologies that might contribute not only to the sustainability of monograph publishing but to the quality of the resulting books' (Willinsky, 2009).

Textbook publishing

Gomez, in *Print is Dead* (2008), traces the history of the relatively slow acceptance of the e-book. Users have had problems with e-readers, reading a full book online, interoperability between providers and prices of e-content. Before the major economic downturn of late 2008, textbooks had already been under pressure from declining student budgets and the Google generation's desire for online 'gobbets' of information. Students used to accessing information and entertainment for free, either through university libraries or via music downloads, are increasingly reluctant to pay significant amounts of money for textbooks, particularly as their economic circumstances decline. The

UK Research Information Network (RIN, 2009) has noted that book purchasing over the past decade has dropped, per FTE student, from £32 to £30 per year.

As student tuition fees increase around the world, the ability or desire on the part of students to buy expensive textbooks diminishes. Business models for textbooks are under as much scrutiny, and experiencing as much change, as the commercial and academic monograph sectors. The State Public Interest Research Groups (SPIRG) in the USA have argued, in *Ripoff 101: how the publishing industry's practices needlessly drive up textbook costs* (SPIRG, 2005), that textbooks are hugely overpriced. With many textbooks in the USA costing over $200, there is considerable resistance to e-book purchase by anyone other than libraries (Eunson, 2009).

The publishing of textbooks has been dominated by a relatively small number of educational publishers. Debus (2008) has provided a historical overview of the educational textbook scene in Australia, highlighting a 'golden era' from the mid 1970s to the mid 1980s. By 2008, however, as detailed in the Australian Society of Authors (ASA) document *Educational Publishing in Australia* (ASA, 2008), publishers had 'drastically reduced terms and conditions offered to authors . . . commercial educational publishing in Australia, for Australia, by Australians no longer works' (Debus, 2008). The ASA report highlights some of the same issues from the SPIRG findings, in that publishers produce expensive add-ons to textbooks, publish editions that differ little from earlier ones, except for adding 'digital ancillaries . . . like the free prawn crackers given away with many Asian take-aways . . . to sweeten the deal'. Debus concludes: 'the business model for educational textbook publishing is broken'.

Given that textbooks are not generally accepted as research output by research assessment bodies, then apart from the relatively few academic authors who still receive substantial royalty payments, the case for an online institutional textbook framework in terms of digital 'mix and match' seems increasingly likely. As the price of college/university textbooks continues to rise, new models, including rental of texts and various open options, will also be explored. Online access is imperative in a 24/7 environment, including library provision to online course pack readings. Links from these to campus learning management systems are essential.

In the UK, the national E-book Observatory Project developed from initiatives by the Joint Information Systems Committee (JISC) E-books Working Group. In 2007 the latter commissioned a report by consultants, which highlighted a number of challenges: 'the key message to come out of the report was that publishers are not making the right textbooks available electronically on the right terms' (Estelle et al., 2009). Ebrary also carried out a global e-book survey, which reported that e-book collections and the research tools they provided were not well understood by a significant percentage of library users. In part, the difficulties reflected confusion with e-book models and problems with interfaces to the collection (2007).

Under the aegis of the E-book Observatory Project, 36 e-books were made available to all UK higher education institutions for the start of the academic year 2007–8. Key points of the usage study, which concluded in December 2008, reveal:

> Sessions typically lasted around 13 minutes and users viewed 6 pages on average of the JISC e-books. . . . The way in which the JISC e-books are being used perhaps indicates that e-books are not being used as a substitute for printed books. 85% of users are spending less than one minute per page. They are using e-books in a non-linear way – dipping in and out. This may indicate that if a user wants to read in a constant, frequent or linear way they will still buy or borrow the printed book. E-books are for 'just in time' or remote use. . . . Students are using e-books in addition to the print they bought or borrowed. Publishers need to recognise that a new pricing model for e-books is required which reflects the actual use and usage behaviour. Library provision of e-books is not a threat but a chance to grow a new market.   (Estelle et al., 2009)

Some academic publishers have called into question the usefulness of existing e-book devices for their target market, claiming that students and researchers need more 'ability to interact' with the internet and other sources. Roger Horton, CEO of Taylor & Francis, has stated that e-book-specific devices were a 'peripheral' part of his business, despite the firm's having produced more than 20,000 e-books: 'Most of our online business is through academic libraries or associated parts of the university, therefore nearly all desk top.' Horton added that digitization was not the main concern, but price and distribution models: 'Of the [Taylor &

Francis] book backlist of some 50,000 titles, over 20,000 are available as e-books (e-book revenues increased 30%) with a print on demand facility for 18,000 titles' (Neilan, 2009).

Ernst (2009), in his 'end-user perspective', states that, from Springer's experience, reading from a computer is still perceived as difficult by many, and print books are still mainly preferred for cover-to-cover reading. The JISC E-books Working Group has also noted some of the issues that have to be resolved by libraries, such as the problems experienced with usage-based models, the fact that students expect to be provided with free access to e-books for their courses, as they have already paid, and that it is still too early to explore OA models for e-books, due to copyright issues.

Publishers need to consider unlimited access subscription models too, given the flows of student demand. Pollock (2009) argues that 'the addition of interactive features such as podcasts online, interaction with Learning Management Systems, and the ability to embed revision notes (flash cards) can increase the e-book's value by offering an enhanced experience to both students and teachers. The personalized experience of e-books also adds a direct-to-student channel to complement the established golden triangle (in the textbook world) of publisher, lecturer and bookseller'.

E-books and facing the music?

While publishers want to retain revenue by strict controls against illegal distribution, users usually want flexibility in price and access. Nothing is set in concrete in terms of user habits, as *Encyclopaedia Britannica* found out. Consumer habits are driven by ease of delivery and economy of scale. The music industry has possible lessons for the book industry, given that the former ultimately encompassed cheaper media and a willingness to let a product be given away for free. If the music industry learned the hard way, in terms of distribution and price, then maybe the publishing industry, outside of the major STM multinationals, who have had a stranglehold on their disciplines to date, has not yet faced the music?

Chris Anderson is the author of the bestselling book *The Long Tail*. He 'dismisses as "a common misunderstanding" the idea that free has ruined the music industry. "Music labels are one tiny bit of the music industry. Every other aspect – the artists, the tours, the merchandise, the licensing – is growing. Only the publishers of the silver discs (that silly old way we used to sell music to consumers) are struggling – and the retailers of those discs." ' (Page, 2009).

Piracy and illegal downloading of e-books is clearly a problem, yet one of the most vexed issues in the debate is digital rights management (DRM). It is perhaps instructive that, since music companies began dropping DRM, sales of legal downloads have risen steadily. In 2004, according to the International Federation of the Phonographic Industry, global downloads were worth $400m (£280m) at retail value, while in 2008 that figure stood at $3.7bn (£2.6bn) (Tivnan, 2009). Most publishers, however, continue to deliver e-book content protected by DRM. Springer is a notable exception, offering 30,000 DRM-free e-books within flat-pricing models based on an institution's size (Ernst, 2009).

The market for e-books, although growing rapidly, is still less than 1% of the total publishing business (Neilan, 2009). Amazon's Bezos believes that an e-book should be substantially cheaper than the print book, a view which has not always been accepted by the traditional publishing industry. In the UK, Hachette plans to sell at 'no more than 10% off the physical price', while Australian publisher Allen & Unwin sells its e-books at approximately 80% of print RRP (Evans, 2009).

So what e-price is right? Again, the jury is still out. But one would have to agree with the Australian Booksellers Association's CEO that 'fundamentally e-books won't work unless they're considerably cheaper than the paper product. The consumer hasn't been trained to expect digital product to be the same prices as physical product' (Evans, 2009). One possible outcome could be a largely free corpus of material, for and from academics and students, within internet frameworks at one end of the e-book spectrum, with both subscription and micropayments at the other. In this respect, there are similarities with trends in the serials area. Key players in these debates will be Google and Amazon. Paul Aiken, the Executive Director of the US Authors Guild, states that ultimately 'there might be one very dominant player who could squeeze most of the profits out of this new market', which 'is frightening for authors and publishers' (Stone and Rich, 2009).

Conclusion

Ray Bradbury once said, in the context of his book *Fahrenheit 451*, 'You don't have to burn books to destroy a culture. . . . Just get people to stop reading them.' What form of reading will be the prevalent form in the 21st century is a moot point. As e-devices increase in efficiency of delivery and they and their content decrease in price, then the modes of transmission will influence patterns of reading behaviour.

However, who will own what we read, and at what price, particularly in the academic world? When I worked in the Bodleian Library, Oxford, new readers had to read an introductory statement which includes the words: 'I hereby undertake not to . . . kindle therein any fire'. Back to *Fahrenheit 451*? The Amazon Kindle reader and Google Book Search both bring many advantages in terms of access to a variety of text and form, but we need at the same time to continue kindling the flames of public access to knowledge to ensure the digital era provides as many opportunities for the freedom of expression as possible.

The challenge for 21st-century scholarship, which includes e-books, is to implement an infrastructure for the digital world untrammelled by the historical legacies in the frameworks and costings of print culture. In academic monograph and textbook production, digital online access will become the norm, more often than not supplemented by data and multimedia additions. Print, however, will not die, given the likely explosion of cheap POD outlets. Readers will still be able to judge a book by its POD cover.

E-book futures are still clearly evolving, and cost and ease of access will be crucial issues. However, a discernible trend is emerging with OA e-book environments. If e-outputs and their impacts become embedded in promotion and tenure and research assessment exercises, then more institutions will assume responsibility for harvesting and providing global access to their scholarship, scholarship that combines authority with public accessibility. A suitable vision for the 21st century? 'Let those who are not old, – who are still young, ponder this well' (Trollope, 1866).

References

AAU (Association of American Universities) et al. (2009) *The University's Role in the Dissemination of Research and Scholarship: a call to action*, www.arl.org/bm~doc/disseminating-research-feb09.pdf.

Alexander, P. H. (2009) What Just Ain't So, *Inside Higher Education*, 6 April, www.insidehighered.com/views/2009/04/06/alexander.

ASA (Australian Society of Authors) (2008) *Educational Publishing in Australia: what's in it for authors?*, www.asauthors.org/lib/pdf/zReports/ASA_Educational_Publishing_Report2008.pdf.

Battles, M. (2009) In Defense of the Kindle, *The Atlantic*, 2 March, www.theatlantic.com/doc/200903u/amazon-kindle-2.

Bauerlein, M. (2009) Relieving Research Expectations in the Humanities, *Inside Higher Education*, 18 March, www.insidehighered.com/news/2009/03/18/production.

Benford, G. (2009) Physics Through Science Fiction. In Gunn, J. (ed.), *Reading Science Fiction*, Palgrave Macmillan.

British Academy (2005) *E-resources for Research in the Humanities and Social Sciences: a British Academy policy review*, British Academy, www.britac.ac.uk/reports/eresources/index.html.

Brown, L., Griffiths, R. and Rascoff, M. (2007) *University Publishing in a Digital Age*, Ithaka Associates, www.ithaka.org/strategic-services/ Ithaka%20University%20Publishing%20Report.pdf.

Carr, N. (2008) Is Google Making us Stupid?, *Atlantic Monthly*, July/August, www.theatlantic.com/doc/200807/google.

Coates, K. (2009) Knowledge Overload, *Inside Higher Education*, 23 March, www.insidehighered.com/views/2009/03/23/coates.

Cox, J. (2008) As I See It!: the future of the printed monograph has arrived, *Against the Grain*, December 2008 to January 2009, www.pc.gov.au/_data/assets/pdf_file/0005/85946/sub268.pdf.

Crane, G. (2009) Tools for Thinking: ephilogy and cyberinfrastructure. In *Working Together or Apart: promoting the next generation of digital scholarship*, CLIR/NEH (Council on Library and Information Resources/National Endowment for the Humanities), www.clir.org/pubs/reports/pub145/pub145.pdf.

Darnton, R. (2009) Google and the Future of Books, *New York Review of Books*, 12 February, www.nybooks.com/articles/22281.

Debus, P. (2008) Publisher, Perish Impoverished, *Australian Author*, 40 (2), 6–10.

Doctorow, C. (2007) Free(konomic) E-Books, *Locus*, 29 September.

Ebrary (2007) *Global eBook Survey*,
www.ebrary.com/corp/collateral/en/Survey/ebrary_eBook_survey_2007.pdf.

Engelhardt, T. (2008) *The Axe, the Book, and the Ad: on reading in an age of depression*,
http://tomdispatch.com/post/175015/the_time_of_the_book.

Epstein, J. (2001) *The Book Business: publishing past, present and future*, W. W. Norton.

Ernst, O. (2009) *The Future of eBooks? Will print disappear? An end user perspective*,
http://conference.ub.uni-bielefeld.de/2009/programme/.

Estelle, L., Milloy, C., Rowlands, I. and Woodward, H. (2009) *Understanding How Students and Faculty REALLY USE E-books: the National E-Books Observatory*. In Mornati, S. and Hedlund, T. (eds), Rethinking Electronic Publishing: innovation in communications paradigms and technologies, *Proceedings of the 13th International Conference on Electronic Publishing, Milan, Italy, 10–12 June*, 381–91,
http://conferences.aepic.it/index.php/elpub/elpub2009/paper/view/79/36.

Ettinghausen, J. (2008) Spine-chilling, *Independent on Sunday*, 14 September,
http://findarticles.com/p/articles/mi_qn4159/is_20080914/ai_n28104865/
pg_6?tag=content;col1.

Eunson, B. (2009) Vexed Future for Set Text, *The Australian Higher Education*, 25 February.

Evans, E. (2009) The e-Price is Right? *Australian Bookseller and Publisher*, (Summer), 9, 32.

Feldman, G. (2009) Bezos Unbound, *The Bookseller*, 13 February,
www.thebookseller.com/blogs/76733-page.html.

Flood, A. (2009) Is this YouTube for Books? *Guardian*, 31 March,
www.guardian.co.uk/books/2009/mar/31/books-scribd-com-ebooks-youtube.

Gomez, J. (2008) *Print is Dead: books in our digital age*, Macmillan, 116–31,
http://books.google.co.uk.

Guevara, S. (2009) *Diving into the Blue: a look at Michigan's repositories*,
www.infotoday.com/cilmag/apr09/Guevara.shtml.

Hahn, K. (2008) Publishing Services: an Emerging Role for Research Libraries,
EDUCAUSE Review, 43 (6), (November/December),
www.educause.edu/ER/EDUCAUSEReviewMagazineVolume43/
PublishingServicesAnEmergingRo/163270.

Hodgkin, A. (2009) Google Book Search and the Tragedy of the Anti-Commons,
ExactEditions, 1 February, http://exacteditions.blogspot.com/2009/02/google-
book-search-and-tragedy-of-anti.html.

Jaschik, S. (2009) Farewell to the Printed Monograph, *Inside Higher Education*, 23 March,
www.insidehighered.com/news/2009/03/23/michigan.

Kingsley, D. A. (2009) *The Effect of Scholarly Communication Practices on Engagement with Open Access: an Australian study of three disciplines*, Australian National University.

Lauerman, J. (2009) MIT Faculty Votes for Free Public Access to Research on Web,
www.bloomberg.com/apps/news?pid=20601103&sid=aoAp1.JFWXE4&refer=us.

Lea, R. (2009) Faber Launches 'Pay-what-you-want' eBook, *Guardian*, 2 March,
www.guardian.co.uk/books/2009/mar/02/faber-ben-wilson-ebook.

Lynch, C. (2005) *The Specialized Scholarly Monograph in Crisis: or how can I get tenure if you won't publish my book?*,
www.arl.org/resources/pubs/specscholmono/Lynch.shtml.

Lynch, C. (2009) *Universities Need to Promote Broader Dissemination of Research and Scholarship*,
www.arl.org/news/pr/universities-12feb09.shtml.

Maron, N. L. and Smith, K. K. (2008) *Current Models of Digital Scholarly Communication*, 5, Association of Research Libraries,
www.arl.org/bm~doc/current-models-report.pdf.

Neilan, C. (2009) E-book Devices 'Not' for Students, *The Bookseller*, 17 March,
www.thebookseller.com/news/79986-e-book-devices-not-for-students.html.

Oder, N. (2009) Harvard's Darnton Asks: is Google the Elsevier of the future? *Library Journal*, 17 March,
www.libraryjournal.com/article/CA6644834.html.

Page, B. (2009) Free Radical, *The Bookseller*, 20 March,
www.thebookseller.com/in-depth/trade-profiles/80519-free-radical.html.

Pinter, F. (2008) Free Thinking at Bloomsbury, *The Bookseller*, 4 December,
www.thebookseller.com/in-depth/trade-profiles/72158-free-thinking-at-bloomsbury.html.

Pollock, D. (2009) JISC Report Gives Insight into E-Book Usage, *Outsell Insights*, 6 April.

RIN (Research Information Network) (2009) *Scholarly Books and Journals at Risk*,
www.rin.ac.uk/files/Scholarly_books_journals_at_risk.pdf.

Robinson, C. (2009) Diary, *London Review of Books*, 26 February, 34–5.

Rosen, C. (2008) People of the Screen, *The New Atlantis*, 22, 20–32,
www.thenewatlantis.com/publications/people-of-the-screen.

Siracusa, J. (2009) *The Once and Future E-book: on reading in the digital age*, http://arstechnica.com/gadgets/news/2009/02/the-once-and-future-e-book.ars/2.

Spate, O. (1979) *The Spanish Lake*, Australian National Library Press.

SPIRG (State Public Interest Research Groups) (2005) *Ripoff 101: how the publishing industry's practices needlessly drive up textbook costs*, 2nd edn, www.maketextbooksaffordable.org.ripoff_2005.pdf.

Steele, C. (1995) *New Romances or Pulp Fiction? Do libraries and librarians have an internet future?* www.ukoln.ac.uk/services/papers/follett/steele/paper.html.

Steele, C. (2008) Scholarly Monograph Publishing in the 21st Century, *Journal of Electronic Publishing*, (Spring), http://quod.lib.umich.edu/cgi/t/text/text idx?c=jep;cc=jep;rgn=main; view=text;idno=3336451.0011.201.

Steele, C., Butler, L. and Kingsley, D. (2006) The Publishing Imperative: the pervasive influence of publication metrics, *Learned Publishing*, 19 (4), 277–90, http://dspace.anu.edu.au/handle/1885/44486.

Stone, B. and Rich, M. (2009) Amazon in Big Push for New Kindle Model, *New York Times*, 9 February, www.nytimes.com/2009/02/10/technology/personaltech/10kindle.html?_r= 1&ref=books y.

Sutherland, J. (2007) Conveyor Belt Criteria, *Guardian*, 18 January, http://education.guardian.co.uk/higher/columnist/story/0,,1993327,00.html.

Swanson, K. (2009) University to Merge Publishing Operations with Library, *The Michigan Daily*, www.michigandaily.com/content/2009-03-24/u-merge-publishing-operations-library.

Thompson, J. B. (2005) Survival Strategies for Academic Publishing, *Chronicle of Higher Education*, 17 June.

Tivnan, T. (2009) Music lessons, *The Bookseller*, 27 February, www.thebookseller.com/in-depth/feature/78675-music-lessons.html.

Trollope, A. (1866) *The Claverings*, chapter 49.

University College London (2009) *The Role and Future of the Monograph in Arts and Humanities Research*, CIBER (Centre for Information Behaviour and Evaulation of Research), www.ucl.ac.uk/infostudies/research/ciber/downloads/monographs.pdf. (See also Williams, P. et al. (2009) The Role and Future of the Monograph in Arts and Humanities Research, *Aslib Proceedings*, 61 (1), 67–82.)

University of Michigan (2009) *U-M Redefining Scholarly Publications in the Digital Age*, 23 March, www.ns.umich.edu/htdocs/releases/story.php?id=7052.

Willes, M. (2008) *Reading Matters: five centuries of discovering books*, Yale University Press.

Willinsky, J. (2009) Toward the Design of an Open Monograph Press, *Journal of Electronic Publishing*, 12 (1), http://quod.lib.umich.edu/cgi/t/text/text-idx?c=jep;cc=jep;rgn=main;view=text;idno=3336451.0012.103.

5

Digitizing the past: next steps for public sector digitization

Alastair Dunning

Where we are now

Barely a week goes by without news of the digital publication of some sparkling cultural resource being splashed across the media – 2009 has been a particularly rich year. 'World's oldest Bible published in full online', reported the *Daily Telegraph* in July 2009, as the website with the Codex Sinaiticus was introduced to the general public (*Daily Telegraph*, 2009).[1] 'Frozen in time: historic images of polar exploration made public', proclaimed the *Daily Mirror*, as the University of Cambridge published its stunning collection of images of early voyages to the Arctic and Antarctic (*Daily Mirror*, 2009).[2] And the *Independent* newspaper marked the launch of the University of Kent's online archive of 20th-century political cartoons by reporting on 'a century of satire, wit and irreverence' (*Independent*, 2008).[3]

Beyond the early blaze of publicity, some digitization projects have proved wildly spectacular, maintaining a considerable audience over time. The Complete Work of Charles Darwin Online, which provides access to numerous digitized documents relating to the naturalist (including several editions of *The Origin of the Species*), claimed 90 million hits between October 2006 and July 2009.[4] The Old Bailey Online, giving extensive details of criminal trials in London's Central Criminal Court from 1674 to 1913, averages 6000 unique visitors a day, which means yearly visitors of just under 2.2 million.[5]

More notoriously, the success of some sites in capturing widespread interest has caused some teething problems. The Vision of Britain site, which provides historic and social information on many places, large and small, in Britain, temporarily crashed after its creator appeared on breakfast TV to promote the site.[6] And the same fate befell The National Archives' 1901 Census site, a fact that really awoke the organization to the huge international interest in the rich seams of genealogical information it holds and proved a springboard for some spectacular digital successes.[7] The blip was only a temporary one for the Vision of Britain site too – it now regularly achieves 80,000 unique users a month.[8]

The issue of sustainability

A casual observer, therefore, might think that this digital world is a well constructed and ordered world. Certainly, the successes mentioned indicate so and deserve praise. Yet the early optimism about digitization has taken something of a battering and revealed a slightly more anarchic digital sphere. The birth of the internet spawned a tiresome flood of clichés and suppositions about presenting digital information online – the belief that knowledge could be instantly democratized via global internet access, that digitization projects were reasonably simple DIY jobs requiring only basic training, that publishing would be cost free via digital means, and that audiences, safely ensconced in their own homes, would flock to see these glittering jewels online. This chapter largely focuses on the UK but the experience has been much the same elsewhere. The report *Shifting Gears* sums up the US experience: 'A lot of money went toward creating barely visited web sites. And a lot of institutions created preservation-quality images that they, in fact, had no way to sustain in the long run' (Erway and Schaffner, 2007, 8).

In the context of publicly funded digitization projects, bitter realities soon disproved many of these uninformed assumptions. In particular, the issue of sustainability – the fact that complex websites require ongoing funding in order to ensure their technical reliability and their intellectual freshness – was the unpleasant jack-in-the-box that kept popping up. Numerous projects received fixed-term funding to digitize, say, their collection of historic architectural photographs and construct a relevant web-enabled database, only to find that they had no funds to tweak and maintain the database, thus threatening its continued online existence. The result was an unhealthy glut of 'error 404' pages.[9]

Much of the detail of these problems was highlighted in a 2007 report, *Digitisation in the UK*, produced by Loughborough University. The report cites an 'impressive accumulation of a body of digital material' but points specifically to 'deep fragmentation in all components of the digitization infrastructure' (Loughborough University, 2005). It offered a range of recommendations, including a UK framework for digitization, the co-ordination of existing services and much greater understanding of user interaction with digitized resources.

Despite the clear direction provided by the Loughborough report, disenchantment seeped into the thinking of the funding bodies that had previously supported digitization. Perhaps the most notable example was the cessation of the Arts and Humanities Research Council's (AHRC's) Resource Enhancement scheme. Running from 2000, the scheme had supported 186 projects to make accessible resources and scholarly information in digital form, including both the Darwin and Codex Sinaiticus projects mentioned above.[10] But it was abruptly stopped in 2007, the review stating that it considered 'the scheme to be ineffective in identifying and addressing gaps in resource provision and meeting the resource needs of the arts and humanities research community'.[11]

Similarly, digitization was pushed down the agenda of the Heritage Lottery Fund (HLF) and the Museums, Libraries and Archives Council (MLA); this may well have been tempered by the experiences of the New Opportunities Fund Digitization Programme (commonly called NOF-digi).[12] Again, there were notable successes here, but despite a glossy review that highlighted them, there appears to have been a feeling that the programme was something of a wasted opportunity: digitization was a complex problem that needed much sophisticated strategic thinking before there could be a serious injection of further public funds.[13]

The JISC Digitisation Programme

At the time of writing (Summer 2009), the Joint Information Systems Committee (JISC – a UK body that supports the use of ICT in higher and further education) is the only UK organization that has provided systematic funding for digitization within recent years. In particular,

Phase 2 of its Digitisation Programme, which ran from 2007 to 2009, learned from many of the mistakes of the past.[14] Whereas earlier programmes had given projects funding and then left them to get on with it, JISC provided much more strategic direction, and funding was conditional on teams addressing each aspect of the digital life cycle. Thus, JISC insisted that each project have sustainability plans in place so as to ensure longevity in the created resources; that each project undertake user analysis and implement marketing and communication plans; and, more generally, that each project be part of a larger digitization community that could share with, advise and learn from the others. The result has been a compelling set of digital resources that seem to be providing a much more systematic return on the initial funding. Time will tell if this approach actually delivers the benefits it aims for. Despite the successes of Phase 2, the economic circumstances of 2009 have meant that there has been no Phase 3 to the Programme; however, JISC has continued its support in the area, providing funding for projects to enhance its existing content or develop the necessary infrastructure for institutions to undertake their own digitization.[15]

Whatever the long-term success or failure of the JISC programme, it is clear that digitization involving public-sector funds requires a far greater degree of high-level strategic implementation than has previously been present. An article in the *Guardian* looking at digitization in the broader context of all content on the internet summarized it nicely with the headline 'Why a Wild West approach just won't do'.[16]

Measures towards sustainability

There are encouraging signs, however, that the complexity of the digitization jigsaw is being considered and pieced together, both in the UK and abroad. The report *Shifting Gears*, produced by the American library service OCLC, alerted the library and information world to the need for changed thinking in the area, pushing forward a provocative series of ideas that challenged previous practice (Erway and Schaffner, 2007). In the southern hemisphere, interesting work in both Australia and New Zealand is taking these agendas forward. In particular, the Digital NZ initiative is providing a strategic focus for all kinds of digital content within New Zealand.[17] And EU funding has also been directed to the development of infrastructure, rather than the digitization of content. For instance, the Impact project is creating a European network of expertise so as to provide a platform for navigating the issues relating to the digitization of text.[18]

Within the UK also moves are similarly afoot. On behalf of the MLA, the Collections Trust is developing CultureGrid as a way of harmonizing existing services and content within the library, museum and archive community.[19] More broadly, the Strategic Content Alliance (SCA), a network of UK public-sector bodies (including primary stakeholders the British Library, the NHS, the BBC, Becta, JISC and the MLA, and a larger number of secondary stakeholders) that share concerns about the long-term issues of access to digital content, is tackling the key issues and encouraging the implementation of the necessary policies.[20]

Perhaps most valuably, a report and series of case studies commissioned by the SCA have begun to shed some light on the bedevilling issue of sustainability. As mentioned above, cultural heritage institutions have struggled with how the staff and the financial support can be found to maintain online resources once the initial project funding has ended. The case studies are particularly enlightening, giving examples of projects, institutions and consortia that have developed the necessary skills and resources to survive in the digital world. These include the Centre for Computing Humanities at King's College London, where a shared technical and human infrastructure has allowed for the deployment of over 80 separate websites of cultural and scholarly content.[21] There are further case studies on, for example, The National Archives' engagement with commercial partners, the harmonization of free and commercial access strategies at the French Institut national de l'audiovisuel, and Cornell University's eBird website, which has harnessed the enthusiasm of amateur ornithologists to create a sustainable resource that meets the needs of both scientists and enthusiasts.[22] In all, the suite of 12 case studies present examples of the more sophisticated approach that will be required to support and sustain digitized content in the future.

Order, but not too much order

The work of the Strategic Content Alliance and others has been a response to the need for greater strategic harmony in the infrastructure that supports public sector digitization. Yet, as a community interested in continuing to explore what digitization can offer, we need to be careful not to instil too much order. While 'anarchy' may be too strong a term, a good dose of breaking established rules and practices will be an integral part of keeping digital content invigorated, helping to reach out to diverse audiences on a global level.

It is worth remembering that earlier digitization programmes were not entirely without a sense of order. Applicants to the AHRC's Resource Enhancement scheme were obliged to fill out a technical appendix which asked for specific information about the technical standards to be used. Those aiming to use proprietary formats (e.g. creating master files in PDF or Microsoft Word) or planning to digitize at an insufficient standard (e.g. photographs as low-resolution JPGs) were asked to rewrite plans to adopt a more open standards approach. Similarly, projects involved in the NOF-digi programme underwent accessibility tests to ensure that their data and websites were being created in accordance with a long list of guidelines developed as part of the programme.[23]

Such an approach undoubtedly had considerable benefits. Data were captured in platform-neutral formats, thus minimizing the chance of images and text becoming trapped in dated software. Websites were presented in a way that did not block access to those who utilized browsers other than the familiar Microsoft Internet Explorer.

But there were drawbacks as well. Such control, particularly in the NOF-digi programme, demanded excessive documentation. More importantly, it placed partial restrictions on those wishing to undertake innovative work and exploit formats that did not fall into the 'canon of openness'.

Barriers to the diffusion of digitized content

But since then there has been much discussion as to the extent to which digitization projects should capture and deliver their data within rigid boundaries. As standards guru Brian Kelly in the UK has documented, an emphasis on standards is to be applauded, but overemphasis ignores the limitations of such a framework (Kelly, Guy and Dunning, 2007). Open standards can be costly, not mature or, as perhaps happens most often, run against the grain of the services and functionality that a general audience expect to see.

The *Shifting Gears* report raised this argument to another level, focusing not just on standards but the whole 'best practice' approach to digital capture. Best practice in digitization has traditionally demanded careful attention to high-resolution capture of rich digital images or other documents, with detailed, hand-crafted metadata lovingly added in as context. To sum up the bullish response of *Shifting Gears* to all this: 'Quality vs. quantity – Quantity wins!' The report identified the marginal position of digitization within library infrastructure and the underuse and subsequent sustainability problem of digital resources as being caused by overly precise methods: 'Our intricate attempts to describe and present a few choice collections have resulted in expensive, but little-used websites. And the rest of our [non-digitized] collections remain largely invisible' (Erway and Schaffner, 2007, 8). To the authors of *Shifting Gears*, slavishly following prescribed guidelines has got in the way of the bigger picture.

However, it is not just best practice, but a whole conceptual approach to digitized content that is still acting as a significant barrier to its wider diffusion. The overwhelming majority of digitization projects have focused on digitizing photographs, drawings, postcards or documents with the intention of delivering them from a custom-made website, which institutions have been responsible for either creating themselves or, at the very least, paying somebody else to create. The result has been to create digital silos – lumps of digital content that cannot be shared, reused or cross-searched without considerable difficulty, even when their content is of a similar nature.

To counter this, there needs to be greater openness, allowing data to be shared, reused and republished, often for purposes different from those for which they were intended. Beyond the sheer quantity of documents that it can digitize, the clear advantage of the Google Books Digitization Programme is that it places the digital content in a web environment (that of Google Search) within which millions of users are already familiar with how the interface operates.[24] There is a much greater chance of a user finding rare books from, for instance, the University of Oxford if they are hosted on a Google website than if they are hidden on the University's ox.ac.uk domain.

In many cases it is quite simple things that restrict the flow of content. For example, the British Library's newspaper digitization programme has created a fantastic resource which, by the end of 2009, should be presenting nearly four million pages to the higher and further educational community and around two million pages to the general public.[25] Yet not only are the URLs that define each newspaper page lengthy and difficult to copy and paste, they alter according to the university or college from where the user hails. Thus, if a lecturer from the University of A wishes to send a reference to a news page to a colleague at B College, he has no immediate way of doing so.

Breaking down boundaries and locating new users

Perhaps more importantly, floating, unstable URLs disrupt the process by which search engines analyse and index individual web pages. Since the majority of users will search for content not by typing a URL in the address bar, but by entering a couple of search terms in Google, blocking search engine access constitutes a wasted opportunity to assist the discovery of a resource.

With sufficient technical planning, problems such as those cited above can be avoided. A more fundamental problem involves the sharing and cross-searching of related digitized resources that exist in different places. For nearly any topic one might choose, one can find numerous digitized resources of relevance scattered across the internet.

A good example is posters relating to World Wars 1 and 2. Posters are an obvious target for digitization, given their fragility, manifest visual appeal and historical importance as primary sources. A significant number of cultural institutions have therefore initiated projects that have included the capture of posters in their collections. Among them are the Imperial War Museum, the University of Minnesota, the University of Oxford, McGill University, the University of Washington and many, many more.[26] Yet there is no convenient way to search across all these collections of posters; indeed, many users may not even know of the existence of these digital collections. Take any other area, such as medieval manuscripts, early photography, documentary films, architectural drawings: painstaking trawling via Google will identify a sprawling archipelago of thematically related digital content.

This is not a new problem. There have been numerous efforts to solve the conceptual issues in bringing together such rich content, often involving the development of portals that either harvest or directly import metadata and then tailor it to provide a functioning cross-search facility. The Vision and Sound Portal based at the EDINA data centre in Edinburgh is just one example, bringing together visual and audio content for use in a higher education context.[27] Such portals have met with partial success, but they have also been expensive, involving much staff time in bringing content partners on board, and the laborious process of squeezing the metadata into the shape required for cross-search functionality.

To begin to overcome this issue, content providers need to become much more undiscriminating in how they allow users to gain access to their content. As mentioned above, previous methods of delivery have focused on making content available via the organization's own website and perhaps also via a portal. But such mechanisms still restrict the contexts in which users can understand and manipulate the content.

New tools and standards for content sharing

There is now a suite of different tools and standards, of varying levels of complexity, that allow cultural content to be harvested, imported, reused and revisualized by global audiences. Content providers should no longer try to confine themselves to one standard by which to make their content available, but should embrace a range of lightweight technologies. Ellis (2009) provides an excellent recapitulation of the issue). Such technologies include RSS, JSON and microformats, and richer standards such as RDF, which form part of the network of ideas that mesh together as the semantic web. Perhaps most importantly, the rise of the API (application programming interface) allows other users to build services and tools based on one's content.[28] The website Flickr is an excellent example, originally conceived as a site for the upload of photographic content. The installation of an API on Flickr allowed for a range of subsidiary services to exploit this interface and build services around it. Users can now create postcards, posters, books and other personalized goods based on the content they have uploaded.[29]

Cultural heritage institutions are now starting to explore the advantages that can be gained from APIs. The Brooklyn Museum in New York is one organization pushing at the boundaries of possibility, and its API has enabled the creation of numerous services that exploit its digital content in different ways.[30] The BBC Backstage project has also focused attention on how developers and others can make use of BBC digital data.[31] Within the academic sphere, Concordia, a shared project between King's College London and New York University, provides a good example. Under development at the time of the writing, the project is exploiting lightweight geographical standards, notably GeoRSS feeds and KML, to integrate different data resources related to the study of classical Africa, mainly inscriptions carved in monuments created during the Roman Empire.[32]

User interactions with digital data

Barring the flow of digital content out to other locations is just one of the traditional boundaries that digitization projects need to break down. How users interact with the digital data is another. Nearly all digitization projects have followed a model in which the holder of knowledge (whether it be university, museum, archive or other) creates the digitized resource, adds the necessary contextual information and presents it to a specific audience for consumption – a model that mimics the one-way flow of information in the lecture hall.

Successful Web 2.0 sites, most notably YouTube and Flickr, have built their foundations on ignoring this model, allowing user-generated content to become the keystone around which their service is delivered. If they are to achieve greater success, future digitization ventures need to question the traditional parameters and develop services that respond to the greater demand for user interaction.

The Great War Archive

Within the UK, perhaps the most successful example of this has been the Great War Archive, an initiative that was born out of a larger project based at the University of Oxford to digitize poetry manuscripts related to World War 1.[33] While the poetry manuscripts were held either by collecting institutions (such as the Imperial War Museum's Isaac Rosenberg collection) or by private estates (such as the manuscript of Wilfred Owen's poem 'Strange Meeting'), the Great War Archive sought to digitize relevant items held by the population at large. Every item originates from, or relates to, someone's experience of World War

1. Members of the public were invited either to submit items in digital form, or to attend special collection days at local libraries where their relevant material was photographed. All material was then uploaded to the website, where it could be searched for either in context with or separately from the material related to the war poets. Additionally, a Flickr group was constituted that enabled further dissemination of the content gathered via the Great War Archive initiative.

The result was overwhelming, and in a few months over 6500 items had been collected, including, according to the project website, 'diaries, photographs, official documents, and even audio interviews with veterans', with hundreds more items added to the Flickr group. As well as offering their own collections to the website, the public were asked to contribute to the metadata, often bringing unique knowledge related to an item that was not to be found elsewhere. But perhaps of even greater value was the broad community of interest that developed around the content, using the websites, joining the Flickr group, commenting on items and, in many cases, supplying authoritative knowledge on the collections presented.

An interesting summary of the project also reveals another eye-catching fact about such digitization projects open to the general public. The report notes that what 'this initiative made clear was the potential for economies of scale that tapping into the potential for mass amateur digitization could produce' (Lindsay, 2009, 21). While each item in the 'official' Poetry Archive cost £40 to develop, publicly contributed digital items in the Great War Archive cost £4 each to create. The report continues: 'Whilst the quality of the items in the Great War Archive could often be questionable, these figures do support the notion that further investigation is warranted to assess the possibilities of engaging the public directly to build community collections that are of educational and historic value' (Lindsay, 2009, 21).

Historic Australian Newspapers

Another notable example of user engagement comes from the National Library of Australia's *Historic Australian Newspapers, 1803 to 1954*.[34] The project is tackling the problem of the somewhat poor results of the automated conversion of newspaper text from physical to digital format (commonly known as optical character recognition, OCR) by inviting members of the public to correct the machine-generated transcripts. One might be sceptical of the enthusiasm of 'an ordinary user' for such a task, but there was an immediate and rapid response from local historians, keen to study and correct texts relating to their own area of interest, often based on particular people or places. The website's 'Text Correctors Hall of Fame' not only provides evidence of the popularity of the task, but helps to generate a gentle sense of rivalry between transcribers.[35]

Conclusion

The dramatic success of these projects should persuade those digitizing resources of the advantages that can be exploited by such an approach. It allows for the collation of more material and engages familiar and new audiences in novel ways. More directly, it should point them to the fact that there is obviously general enthusiasm to engage with culture on a digital sphere. This, of course, does not mean that the digital should replace the physical institution. Neither should such work be undertaken without due consideration of how it affects the institution's image as a trusted place of learning, nor exaggerate the extent to which there is educational demand for information relating to individual families' histories.[36] But such methods of user engagement indicate the innovative ways in which digitized content can enhance the cultural and learning experience that universities, libraries and the like area are trying to provide.

It is perhaps a little too strong to label these concerns for opening up data, breaking down boundaries and locating new users as a call for anarchy. At best, it is a call to dissolve some of the frontiers that digitizing institutions have inherited whilst thinking about their collections as physical entities. Rather than keep it locked in a single place to which users must come and visit, there is need for digitized content to be dispersed on the internet, passing through as many channels as possible. And beneath all this, there is still a need for sophisticated forms of organization to underpin the delivery of digitized material. The lessons from earlier digitization work still need to be fully digested and, more importantly, acted upon by all the relevant stakeholders. Creating the necessary structures, often in partnership, where institutions can build, deliver and curate their digital content will require a considerable amount of well organized planning and execution.

Notes

1 The manuscript is available from www.codexsinaiticus.org/en/.

2 The polar photographs are available at www.freezeframe.ac.uk.

3 The Cartoon Archive is available at www.cartoons.ac.uk/.

4 Figures cited at the home page of http://darwin-online.org.uk/.

5 Tim Hitchcock, Robert Shoemaker, *Digitising History from Below*, https://uhra.herts.ac.uk/dspace/bitstream/2299/38/1/102846.pdf. The Old Bailey site is available at www.oldbaileyonline.org/.

6 The site is available at www.visionofbritain.org.uk/.

7 See www.1901censusonline.com/. Details about the crash are at http://news.bbc.co.uk/1/hi/uk/1749045.stm.

8 Unpublished project report for Historic Boundaries of Britain project, page 1.

9 The 404 error is the message given by a browser when it can no longer find a webpage. http://en.wikipedia.org/wiki/HTTP_404.

10 A list of these projects is available at http://web.me.com/xcia0069/ahrc.htmls.

11 www.ahrc.ac.uk/FundedResearch/Pages/ResourceEnhancementSchemeReview. aspx. The full report does not appear to be publicly available. Other relevant research in the area is available from www.ahrcict.rdg.ac.uk/activities/strategy_projects/reports/index.htm.

12 There is a useful blog post on this at http://bridgetmckenzie.blogspot.com/2008/05/mla-and-hlf-views-on-21st-c-curation.html.

13 For a summary of the programme see Woodhouse (2001). The final evaluation report, published by consultants Education for Change in 2006, is at www.biglotteryfund.org.uk/er_eval_ict_final_rep.pdf.

14 The list of 22 projects funded by JISC within Phase 1 (2004–7) and Phase 2 (2007–9) of its Digitisation Programme are at www.jisc.ac.uk/whatwedo/programmes/digitisation/projects.aspx. A full list of all digitization projects funded by JISC since 2004, including its 2008–9 Enriching Digital Resources strand (which provided short bursts of funding to enhance existing digital content), is at http://web.me.com/xcia0069/jisc.html.

15 http://digitisation.jiscinvolve.org/2009/07/03/does-jisc-have-funds-for-more-digitisation/;www.jisc.ac.uk/fundingopportunities/funding_calls/2009/02/grant0 209econtent.aspx.

16 http://education.guardian.co.uk/librariesunleashed/story/0,,2274844,00.html.

17 www.digitalnz.org/about.

18 www.impact-project.eu/home/.

19 http://openculture.collectionstrustblogs.org.uk/2009/04/27/culture-grid-starts-to-take-shape/.

20 www.jisc.ac.uk/contentalliance.

21 www.ithaka.org/ithaka-s-r/strategy/ithaka-case-studies-in-sustainability/case-studies/SCA_BMS_CaseStudy_CCH.pdf.

22 All 12 case studies are available from www.ithaka.org/ithaka-s-r/strategy/ithaka-case-studies-in-sustainability.

23 The original guidelines were present on the People's Network site, but the URL (www.peoplesnetwork.gov.uk/content/technical.asp) no longer functions. The support service run by the UKOLN and the Arts and Humanities Data Service had a (still functioning) website at www.ukoln.ac.uk/nof/support/.

24 http://books.google.com/.

25 www.bl.uk/britishnewspapers.

26 A good list is at www.oucs.ox.ac.uk/ww1lit/education/online/propaganda.html.

27 A useful final report highlights some of the key obstacles in creating the portal: http://edina.ac.uk/projects/vsmportal/docs/VSMFinalReport.pdf. In the USA, the Aquifer initiative (www.diglib.org/aquifer/) has looked at tackling many of the same issues. There are many others.

28 http://en.wikipedia.org/wiki/Application_programming_interface.

29 www.flickr.com/do/more/.

30 www.brooklynmuseum.org/opencollection/api/. The news link from this URL gives examples of the different ways in which the API has been exploited, e.g. creating applications for the iPhone, or various different interfaces which look at particular aspects of the collection.

31 http://backstage.bbc.co.uk/.

32 http://concordia.atlantides.org/. Information on the standards is available at http://en.wikipedia.org/wiki/GeoRSS and http://en.wikipedia.org/wiki/KML.

33 The First World War Poetry Digital Archive is available at www.oucs.ox.ac.uk/ww1lit/, and the Great War Archive is embedded within this at www.oucs.ox.ac.uk/ww1lit/gwa/. The Flickr group for the Great War Archive is at www.flickr.com/groups/greatwararchive/.

34 http://ndpbeta.nla.gov.au/.

35 http://ndpbeta.nla.gov.au/ndp/del/hallOfFame. The Old Bailey Online project has also developed a wiki (www.hrionline.ac.uk/obp-wiki/index.php/Main_Page), which allows users to add contextual information, for example 'biographical material about individuals and families who are documented in the Old Bailey Proceedings and Ordinary's Accounts'.

36 To consider these issues, JISC has commissioned Chris Batt Consulting to undertake a feasibility study on the digitization and curation of collections from the general public. The results will be available at www.jisc.ac.uk/whatwedo/programmes/digitisation/reports/digicuration.aspx from Autumn 2009.

References

Daily Mirror (2009) *Frozen in Time: historic images of polar exploration made public*, 4 March, www.mirror.co.uk/news/top-stories/2009/03/04/frozen-in-time-historic-images-of-polar-exploration-made-public-115875-21170538/.

Daily Telegraph (2009) *World's Oldest Bible Published in Full Online*, 6 July, www.telegraph.co.uk/news/newstopics/religion/5749555/Worlds-oldest-Bible-published-in-full-online.html.

Ellis, M. (2009) *Don't Think Websites, Think Data*, www.slideshare.net/dmje/dont-think-websites-think-data.

Erway, R. and Schaffner, J. (2007) *Shifting Gears: gearing up to get into the flow*, report produced by OCLC Programs and Research, www.oclc.org/programs/publications/reports/2007-02.pdf.

Independent (2008) *A Century of Satire, Wit and Irreverence*, 3 November, www.independent.co.uk/news/media/online/a-century-of-satire-wit-and-irreverence-986844.html.

Kelly, B., Guy, M. and Dunning, A. (2007) *Addressing the Limitations of Open Standards*, www.archimuse.com/mw2007/papers/kelly/kelly.html.

Lindsay, K. (2009) *First World War Poetry Archive Final Report*, www.jisc.ac.uk/media/documents/programmes/digitisation/ww1finalreport.pdf.

Loughborough University (2005) *Digitisation in the UK*, www.jisc.ac.uk/whatwedo/programmes/digitisation/reports/digiukframework.aspx.

Woodhouse, S. (2001) The People's Network and the Learning Revolution: building the NOF digitise programme, *Ariadne*, 29, www.ariadne.ac.uk/issue29/woodhouse/.

6

Resource discovery

Graham Stone

Introduction

Today's researchers use a wide variety of tools to discover the information resources they require. These resources may be located within a physical library or available on the web and, if so, are available in a proliferation of formats and interfaces, which has often meant that users were directed to a number of different in-house or external systems to find the information they required. Over the past ten years libraries have, to a varying degree, sought to manage and expose this data, while attempting to dissuade users from flocking to the simplicity of Google (Scholar), Amazon, YouTube, etc. However, the provision of these different resource-discovery systems uses an increasing amount of the resources in today's academic library.

A review of the recent literature suggests that users prefer simple search interfaces such as Google (Nicholas et al., 2009). The implication here is that libraries often fail to make their resources discoverable and that this may in turn affect the perceived value of the library.

In a recent report for vice-chancellors and senior institutional managers the Research Information Network (RIN) stated that:

> The usefulness of the content and collections provided by libraries and from other sources depends on how easily researchers can discover, locate and gain access to them. Institutions need to ensure that their researchers can readily make use, through the library and other

providers, of services that enable them to discover, locate and gain access to information sources that may be relevant to their research.

(RIN, 2008)

However, do libraries have a sufficient understanding of their users to provide this level of support in the way the libraries users expect and demand? Is there a very real danger of information overload from the plethora of different systems or lack of intuitive interfaces driving users towards Google? Is this actually a problem? In a time of severe fiscal hardship how can libraries restore their importance and reclaim their position?

This chapter looks at both traditional methods of resource discovery and the next-generation systems entering the marketplace in 2009 and asks if these will be appropriate in the next five to ten years.

Abstract and indexing databases

40% of university libraries plan cuts to book and journal purchases next year.   (Corbyn, 2009)

The current financial climate has led many academic libraries to question their resource budgets. With a significant decrease in the amount of expenditure on books as a proportion of the library budget (HCSTC, 2004), and evidence from CIBER (Centre for Information Behaviour and the Evaluation of Research) suggesting that a further cut in journal budgets may have serious effects on universities' research capabilities (CIBER, 2009), libraries will have to look to other areas of the information fund to make the required cuts, and traditional abstracting and indexing (A&I) databases are an obvious choice.

Quality vs Cost

It is not necessarily suggested that the culling of all A&I databases is the answer. In fact, this would prove detrimental to resource discovery in the digital world. Librarians have a duty to give their users a wide variety of resource discovery options, which must include the potential to discover research that lies outside the libraries' full-text holdings. However, gone are the days when a library could afford to subscribe to a wide variety of A&I databases on a similar subject; the library must choose the right amount of resources, depending on the perceived quality of these resources, available budgets and the needs of the users.

Over the next few years every A&I database must show value for money. Quality is not just about accuracy of data. Any A&I database that does not include the following is at risk of cancellation:

Article abstracts: many A&I databases are still only indexes, e.g. one or two sentences of text describing the article. This is often frustrating to the user.

Cover to cover indexing: although many databases list a large number of journal titles in their coverage, further inspection often reveals that this is split between core content (cover to cover indexing); secondary content (where more than 50% of the material is indexed); and tertiary content (where less than 50% of the material is indexed). Any A&I database with a low proportion of core content or a high proportion of tertiary content is at risk.

Full-text linking: an A&I database that effectively sends users down a cul-de-sac, by not linking or providing the means through OpenURL linking (see below) to access external full text, does not promote resource discovery.

Date coverage: unless specifically covering an archive period, A&I databases that purport to be current, but index a high number of ceased titles, are arguably less relevant to users and provide little value for money.

Geographical coverage: often research requires information from specific geographical areas; if these are not adequately covered, then the resource is not valuable for research.

Publisher coverage: libraries want to use A&I databases to achieve a good spread of publishers; if a database does not achieve this, then the resource is little better than searching a publisher's platform. Clearly, this spread may be dependent on subject.

Intuitive interface: is the resource as easy to use as Google? If not, users may go elsewhere.

Shibboleth authentication, EZProxy access as standard: any A&I database that relies on individual user names and passwords for access is creating a barrier to use.

Unrestricted access: analysis of turnaways and usage data at the University of Huddersfield shows that resources that restrict access by number of simultaneous users often have a dramatic drop in usage over a period of time as users become frustrated by turnaway messages. In addition, restrictions by location, e.g. campus use/overseas, also result in potential low usage.

COUNTER-compliant usage data: libraries are often suspicious of resources that do not reveal usage data, or become frustrated when lack of compliance with the COUNTER code of practice for usage statistics (see www.projectcounter.org) means that accurate comparisons cannot be made.

Federated search, as a minimum: services that cannot be added to the federated or harvested search (see below) are effectively making their resources invisible to today's user, who expects a 'just in time' approach to resource discovery.

Another issue is duplication of content. If funds do not permit the number of A&I databases we have been used to in recent years, then two resources with similar content are not economically justifiable. The JISC (Joint Information Systems Committee) Academic Database Assessment Tool (ADAT)[1] allows some of the above comparisons to be made with a limited number of A&I and full-text databases. However, simple manipulation of A&I database title lists in Excel (title lists are available on most vendor websites) can pay dividends, especially when looking at duplication of titles across a range of products.

Citation databases

Citation databases are a different beast. As long as citation rates and impact factors are important in research assessment across the world – and early indication in the UK for the Research Excellence Framework (REF)[2] suggests that there will be an element of peer review informed by bibliometrics in the 2014 exercise – then citation databases will be required as standard by universities with a research interest.

Indeed, citation databases may well have a significant impact on other smaller, 'general' A&I databases that are already at risk of cancellation, as they have introduced a number of enhancements over the past few years:

- Cross-referencing between ProQuest CSA (Cambridge Scientific Abstracts) and Scopus, available since 2007, allowing reciprocal searching, linking and de-duplicating of 4500 CSA titles in Arts & Humanities and Social Sciences and 4500 Scopus titles in Natural Sciences and Business & Economics.[3] This fills a noticeable gap for Scopus in Arts & Humanities and Social Sciences coverage.
- The announcement of Thomson Reuters Links Article Match Retrieval Service in 2009, which allows subscribers to Web of Science or Journal Citation Reports (JCR) to gain easier access to data, such as citation counts, in order to enhance institutional repositories, etc. Subscribers to JCR can use this service to retrieve links to the record for a given journal,[4] allowing a real-time lookup of bibliographic metadata such as digital object identifier (DOI), author, source title, etc., against the Web of Science database. If a match is found, the service will return times cited information as well as links to view the full record, related records page, or citing articles page in Web of Science.
- The further announcement in 2009 that Serials Solutions' Summon Service will feature Web of Science citing references.[5]

However, in 1997 Cameron suggested an alternative to the subscription database, where

> [o]ne approach towards the development of a universal (or semi-universal) citation database would be the establishment of a consortium of universities, academic societies and research library associations devoted to the purpose. . . . A universal citation database would have considerable value as a tool for both literature research and the evaluation of scholarly work and hence could act as a strong catalyst for overall reform in scholarly communication. . . . Indeed, a net savings may be achieved by rational and integrated reallocation of existing resources presently devoted to bibliography preparation, curriculum vitae maintenance and literature indexing. (Cameron, 1997)

Canós et al. (2009) take this research a stage further by suggesting that citation data should be considered part of the scientific community's heritage, and that current technology is available to allow the 'existence of a global, community-maintained citation registry, generated via the early collection of citation data' and that this would be a viable replacement for commercial systems. Any implementation of this technology could create a sea change over five to ten years.

Primary material

So far this chapter has concentrated largely on secondary sources of information. Previously, primary sources of information, such as diaries, speeches, documents and raw data have been more difficult to trace; however, in a digital environment this information is becoming more retrievable.

The work of the JISC Digitisation Programme[6] has created an extensive source of primary material in the UK since 2004, with 22 projects already funded[7] and a further 25 projects nearing completion as part of the Enriching Digital Resources strand.[8]

In addition, the UK Research Data Service Feasibility Study final report (UKRDS, 2008) highlights that over the past ten years research data has remained a 'substantially untapped resource' and that it is 'often unstructured and inaccessible to others'. The report goes on to note that similar views have been expressed internationally, in the USA and Australia.

The challenge over the next five to ten years is for universities to collate and audit this data[9] and make it available either through a centralized facility or through university repositories.

Persistent identifier systems

'Error 404 - page not found'

> The main frustration is not with the research discovery services themselves but with the problem of subsequently accessing identified sources and materials. The last mile of the process which actually delivers the document or other source that has been searched for is the focus of concern, with lack of access to journal articles because of a subscription barrier being the most frequently-expressed difficulty experienced. Librarians agree with researchers that the key problem is accessing online journals rather than problems with the discovery tools themselves. (RIN, 2006)

Persistent identifiers (PIs) attempt to solve the problems of location-based identifiers such as the uniform resource locator (URL), which can often lead to problems in accessing resources, caused by the resource being moved, relocated or renamed while external links to the resource remain unchanged. PIs give the resource a unique identifier that will not change over time, allowing for reliable referencing and access.

Emma Tonkin (2008) identifies a number of standards 'at a mature stage in development':

- the Uniform Resource Name (URN)
- the persistent URL (PURL); the Handle system
- the digital object identifier (DOI)
- National Bibliography numbers (NBNs)
- the Archival Resource Key (ARK)
- the OpenURL.

The JISC Standards Catalogue[10] gives a detailed explanation of these standards, including those listed above and many others. For the purposes of resource discovery, this chapter will concentrate on the DOI and the OpenURL.

Digital Object Identifier (DOI)

> The DOI System was developed as a cross-industry, cross-sector, not-for-profit effort managed by an open membership collaborative development body, the International DOI Foundation (IDF) founded in 1998.[11]

The DOI could be described as the telephone number of a journal article; however, like any telephone number, it needs a directory in order to be discovered. In the case of scholarly content, this directory service is provided by CrossRef, the official DOI link registration agency for scholarly and professional publications. Each record in the CrossRef database consists of a triplet: {metadata + URL + DOI} in order to facilitate resource discovery.[12]

Since the foundation of CrossRef, over 2800 publishers have participated, adding over 20,000 journals and e-books. This resource has proved crucial to resource discovery, in that citations listed in journal articles and institutional repositories have become instantly traceable. Many article citations now come from the author complete with a DOI, something that was brought to many researchers' attention when DOIs were required by the 2008 UK Research Assessment Exercise (RAE).[13]

However, an issue with DOIs is that, despite many publishers' listing an article as having a DOI, not all of them are actually registered at CrossRef, which can lead to frustration. Essentially, if the item cannot be found in CrossRef, the article becomes harder to retrieve. In addition, the DOI will typically link to the publisher's site, which does not guarantee access at the point of use. For example, if the library has a subscription to the article via an intermediary, then the DOI will be of no use for resource discovery; this is known as the appropriate copy problem (Beit-Arie et al., 2001).

OpenURL

> An OpenURL enables the transfer of metadata about an item (a journal article or book, for example) from a resource, where a citation is discovered (for example, an Abstracting & Indexing (A&I) database), to a link resolver. By providing a means to tell another system *what* something is, rather than *where* it is located on the internet (the function of a normal URL), OpenURLs provide a means for link resolvers to take charge of directing users at particular institutions or organisations to appropriate, subscribed resources for the content, be they in electronic or print form.
> (Culling, 2007)

Originally developed as part of a research project by Herbert Van de Sompel and Patrick Hochstenbach at Ghent University (Van de Sompel, Hochstenbach and Beit-Arie, 2000), the OpenURL is now an NISO Standard (NISO, 2004); however, Culling, in his 2007 report (Culling, 2007) to the UKSG,[14] which explored the data supply chain that has developed in recent years to facilitate the creation of link resolver knowledge bases, identified a number of issues and barriers such as:

- lack of understanding and close co-operation by stakeholders
- a significant number of stakeholders that do not make their

collection details available
- lack of open engagement and transparency regarding knowledge base requirements
- lack of understanding as to the use to which the data will be put, leading to inaccuracy
- accuracy not being a major concern of full-text aggregators
- competition between organizations hindering data sharing
- lack of clarity and transparency regarding standards, frequency of data updates and linking syntaxes
- the absence of a code of practice and information standards to ensure optimal knowledge base compliance in addition to the OpenURL.

FRBRization

If an A&I database or institutional repository does not have a direct link to DOI or OpenURL, or the ability to add this information via a link resolver product in order to link to full-text content (whether subscribed or not), that record is of little use to today's researcher. In addition, any publisher (and there are many) who does not register a DOI or an OpenURL to all articles, including editorials, etc., will perpetuate the barriers to resource discovery. Those that register the DOI but do not display either it or the OpenURL on the page effectively render themselves 'ex-directory' as far as repository managers are concerned, as trying to trace a DOI via CrossRef using citation details can prove frustrating.

Separately, the DOI and OpenURL have gone a long way to satisfying the different needs of the community; however, in their 2006 article Apps and MacIntyre ask whether 'incorporating a DOI within an OpenURL, where available, will take advantage of the exact resolution capabilities of DOI'. This could be crucial when looking to the future, where the FRBRization[15] (Functional Requirements for Bibliographic Records: the creation of a set of records that all represent the same work rather than a display that shows all the different editions separately) of records in metasearch and other discovery services would enable an article that might be held in the repository, indexed in an A&I database, and held in full text through a journal publisher's site or via an intermediary, to be displayed as one record.

Meyer reported that 59% of readers in a survey by Canada's National Research Council wanted linking from references to cited articles (Meyer, 2008). However, reference quality and accuracy have been weaknesses in scholarly publishing for many years. Meyer goes on to describe a number of areas of best practice for publishers, including checking references earlier in the submission process. In addition, A&I databases can include incorrect citations; a quick search of one database in preparation for the opening section of this chapter revealed 18 records, one of which led the author to the wrong issue of the required journal.

In 1998 Tim Berners Lee suggested that 'Cool URIs don't change' (Berners Lee, 1998); however, over ten years later, PIs are not routinely applied, and this is essential in the digital information world.

The key to resource discovery

In January 2008 UKSG and NISO jointly launched the Knowledge Bases And Related Tools working group (KBART)[16] to:

1 Develop and publish guidelines for best practice to effect smoother interaction between members of the knowledge base supply chain. Knowledge base providers and their customers (primarily academic libraries) will benefit from provision of higher quality data by content providers. Publishers will benefit from accurate linking to their content and subsequently the possibility of increased usage.

2 Provide educational events that will address the roles of each (relevant) party in the supply chain, the functions each needs to carry out to improve supply of data to knowledge bases, and the value of doing so in each case. Content providers will benefit from a greater understanding of the needs and activities of those to whom they supply data; knowledge base providers and libraries will again benefit from improvements that can be expected when content providers are better educated.

3 Deliver a centralised information portal, to support educational activities and provide a comprehensive resource for further learning.   (www.niso.org/workrooms/kbart)

The KBART Report from February 2009 indicated that progress is being made:

> We've also recently held discussions with CrossRef about how they can complement KBART's work by providing related services to their members. CrossRef will likely proceed with developing a service that offers to collate its members' KBART-related data for onward distribution to, or collection by, link resolver managers.[17]

The success of this working group is essential if resource discovery is to overcome the present barriers.

Federated (meta) searching

> The jury is still out on federated search systems, even though more libraries now have them. There are murmurings that federated search has lower-than-expected use and may not be the magic search bullet we were led to believe. (Tenopir, 2007)

Federated searching (or meta searching) is now a mature product, having been with us now for over ten years,[18] during which time a number of products have come and gone from the marketplace. However, is it the Holy Grail[19] that we were once led to believe it was?

Many librarians do not recommend federated search, despite actual usage increasing (King, 2008). Anecdotal evidence from users' comments at the University of Huddersfield concurs. Problems with federated search rank alongside lack of library textbooks as the perennial favourite in the students' comments. So what are the arguments for and against?

Benefits

Simultaneous search: possibly the very reason many libraries purchased federated searches in the first place – an opportunity to take the fight to Google.

Personalization features: the ability to personalize database and e-journal lists and to save searches are seen as benefits for the federated search.

OpenURL: integration with an OpenURL resolver is an essential part of any resource discovery platform.

Disadvantages

Cross-database search: users do not inherently know which databases to search when faced with having to search each one individually. Although meta-search systems allow users to search multiple databases simultaneously, that does little in itself to resolve the question of why a user would choose to search, say, Project Muse and JSTOR simultaneously over WorldCat and Academic Search Elite (Walker, 2007). Walker argues that in order to allow users to customize their searches, librarians are in fact reverting to old style lists.

Non-searchable content: no federated search can search all subscribed databases for a number of reasons: permission is withheld by the vendor, the resource is not compatible with federated search, or there is a restriction on access, e.g. simultaneous users, username/password access. In some cases, e.g. law, this can render federated searching of little use; this may result in the federated search being very difficult to market from the librarian's point of view.

Dumbing down: the limited search capability means that controlled vocabulary, indexes or thesauri, or in some cases even date-range or peer-review filters, are lost to the federated searcher. This may result in the possibility of inferior results; again, this often discourages librarians from marketing federated searching to certain users, e.g. researchers, faculty.

Lack of direct links to full-text content: although it is no more than a few clicks away using the OpenURL resolver, the federated search still returns no more full-text content than searching A&I databases individually. This is one of the main reasons why librarians at the University of Huddersfield do not recommend federated searching for undergraduates who require full text immediately.

Speed: a federated search is only as fast as the slowest database to retrieve results and therefore, when searching across a range of databases, federated searches have a tendency to extreme slowness or even timing out, and this does little to promote this method of resource discovery.

Interface too complex, not intuitive: faculty and researchers have their favourite databases, and librarians will quickly be able to recommend a top three resources by subject; the federated search brings a new, unfamiliar and perhaps unwieldy interface to the user for all the reasons stated above.

Not Google-like enough: although the prospect of a one-stop shop is tempting, federated searches do not find a variety of material that can be of use to the researcher, e.g. this chapter references a number of blogs and web pages, and how discoverable is this data? For almost as long as Google has been in existence, librarians have been fighting it, but it does have its uses! In addition, institutional repositories using Open Archives Initiative Protocol for Metadata Harvesting (OAI-PMH) can be cross-searched, but this is very basic and is unavailable in federated searches. This could mean that Open Access via a university repository to a search result is not evident.

Are academic librarians correct in their assumptions (Lampert and Dabbour, 2007)? Of course, the real answer to this is usability testing. The historical answer to providing resource discovery for users was to duplicate lists in the library catalogue, web pages, meta-search products, A–Z lists, etc.; no wonder, then, that federated searching has proved popular as users require a one-stop shop approach (Helfer and Wakimoto, 2007).

Tenopir (2007) stated that '[f]ederated systems remain controversial because they focus on what we think users want, at the expense of functionality, precision, and finesse. They are still a long way from providing a single, simple solution to information retrieval.' Given that usability testing shows that the idea of a one-stop shop is popular in principle with students, but the concept is unpopular with librarians, is federated searching a transient technology, like the CD-ROM, and is the real Holy Grail just over the horizon?

Pre-harvested search – the true one-stop shop?

> The second major approach to federated search is to harvest all of the relevant sources of data, normalize them into a single metadata schema, and index all of them together in one large union index. This approach offers huge advantages in speed and in the logic that can be applied to the presentation and sorting of results.
>
> (Gibson, Goddard and Gordon, 2009)

Since January 2009 a number of products have been announced for beta or open beta testing, the big three being Serials Solutions' Summon Service,[20] Ex-Libris' Primo[21] and OCLC's Worldcat Local.[22] These products intend to move a step beyond traditional federated search products in creating a union index solution by harvesting content. They present a new generation of resource discovery by attempting to provide the best bits of federated search while eliminating the downside:

Single search: a Google-like search box.

Relevancy ranking: by using open-source algorithms such as Lucene, these products rank results so that relevant results, rather than the results from the quickest database, appear at the top; this provides quality of search results, rather than the quantity of a Google search.

Hosting: these services offer hosted support on centralized servers.

Integration: open APIs are used in order to integrate the products with existing library systems or next-generation catalogues such as VuFind, etc.

Clustering and faceting: these features are easier to implement with a hosted union index.

Full text and peer review: results can be limited to full-text and/or peer-reviewed content only, finally allowing fast full-text scholarly results to be displayed for the user.

'Did you mean' suggestions: guidance for alternative spellings, misspellings and results with low hits.

Union Index

The harvested data does not only cover A&I databases; the library finally has the opportunity to add local holdings information, such as the library catalogue (including real-time loans information), the institutional repository, and locally and nationally digitized primary material. This in turn creates the potential to allow libraries to avoid duplicating their own lists; for example, if the majority of the library's e-journal and e-book holdings are directly searchable in the pre-harvested index, either through full-text availability via publishers' websites or aggregators, or via OpenURL from databases and institutional repositories, the need for this information through A–Z lists and library catalogues is minimal.

Can we really move away from A–Z lists completely? Can the library catalogue revert to being to a record of the print holdings in the library, essentially a facet of the union index? There are certainly benefits to the idea of a union index for resource discovery; however, there is still some debate as to whether this is the right choice:

> The danger with relying on any one service to provide you with access
> to its indexed content is that the service's criteria for source selection
> may not be yours. (Lederman, 2009)

However, a counter-argument is that users of federated searching do not necessarily choose A&I databases either. Indeed as highlighted by Rochkind (2009) in his reply to the above blog post: 'EVERY SINGLE content provider does NOT make their content available for federated search in the first place. Of the approximately 800 licensed databases we have listed in our collection, only about 300 are federated searchable. The remainder are largely not there because of lack of functionality on the content provider's end, not on our fed search vendor's end.' In fact the recent press release from Serials Solutions seems to indicate that some content is more readily available to harvested search than to federated search.[23]

Indeed, Google does not index everything on the web, but it indexes a lot. No tool for uncovering academic information is entirely comprehensive in its coverage. Research at Stockholm University shows that students were not enthusiastic about Google Scholar or MetaLib; however, they agreed that Google Scholar was easy to use (Nygren et al., 2006).

Compare the market

The success of the new breed of 'web discovery services' will be seen over the next five to ten years; however, the fact that three of the major players have all thrown their hats into the ring shows that they must believe there is significant benefit in developing such systems. It will be up to libraries to gauge whether the benefits of harvested search outweigh those of federated search (Lederman, 2008).

Libraries will need to plan their e-resources strategies accordingly, before assessing this new market, by developing a plan to see where they want to be in five years' time and mapping out the journey for how they want to get there. Libraries need to prioritize which of the benefits of harvested/federated search are most important:

- a first-class search engine for your users
- increased user satisfaction
- increased usage
- a single interface
- 'one-stop shop' approach
- improved system management (interoperability and flexibility)
- mix and match
- future-proofing
- improved system management (management and administration)
- less duplication of effort/more efficiencies
- better control of subscriptions
- improved value for money
- within existing budget.

The order of these priorities should influence the terms of reference and will therefore assist in weighting any evaluation of products and services (Laurisden and Stone, 2009).

With neither solution, as yet, providing a search of all A&I content, a switch from federated to harvested search may, in reality, mean a switch from one set of incomplete resources to another. However, in the long run, users will choose the method of resource discovery that they prefer.

Understanding our users

The change in user behaviour as users move towards a fully digital library brings about a real possibility that librarians and libraries will become removed from their users (Nicholas, 2008). However, this change in behaviour also creates an opportunity to collect user information and to monitor use; Walker (2009) likens this to being seated on a goldmine.

Text and data mining

Unlike the physical library, where little objective information could be gleaned from irregular usage checks, it is no longer satisfactory to think that we know what is best for the user. We can utilize usage statistics to inform us of the potential value of a given resource, but we can also look much deeper into how users behave: which sites do they refer from, how long do they stay, what do they do when they are there, where do they go? This allows librarians to make informed decisions (CIBER, 2007). It does not mean to say that we cannot select or recommend what the user may need, but we must do it in an informed way, and in their language.

At the University of Huddersfield, Web 2.0-style recommender services and usage logs are being used to create additional features on the library catalogue to enhance resource discovery (Pattern, 2009a). Although some of this functionality refers to both electronic and print resources, it should be noted that for many subjects print is (and will continue to be) a major source of much of the scholarly content and is therefore crucial to resource discovery, even in a digital world:

Zero hits: accounted for 23% of searches over a six-month period; this now automatically generates a 'did you mean . . .', '. . . or maybe' spell checker and 'serendipity searches'. The serendipity search generates suggestions by running the search against a number of external reference websites (including www.answers.com). The results returned from these sites are then compared against the catalogue to generate a series of potentially relevant keyword searches. Users are then invited to use their own judgement to decide whether or not the suggested searches (and also the results they generate) are relevant to the original search.

Renew prompt: during the six months' analysis of keyword searches, the word 'renew' was entered 74 times. The following text now appears to aid the user: 'To renew items you currently have on loan, please click on the "My Account/Renewals" tab.'

Tag cloud: a visual depiction of the most popular keywords from the last two days; although the data often carries the same basic set of keywords, there are interesting anomalies throughout the year.

People who borrowed this also borrowed: analysis of borrower history has led to the creation of a suggestions list for additional material.

Items with similar subject headings: in order to give suggestions for similar items.

Other editions: using web services from OCLC[24] and LibraryThing[25] to locate other editions and related works within the holdings.

E-mail alerts and RSS (Really Simple Syndication) feeds: to help users monitor new items added in their areas of research.

ticTOCS: The Journal Tables of Contents Service (ticTOCS) has made its data available, so it is now possible to add links to journal RSS feeds direct from the catalogue.[26]

User rating and comments: are available to add from the record.

Loans per year: are available for all print copies for users to gauge the popularity of the items.

Google Book Search: to allow users to sample a book online before they borrow/reserve it.

There is anecdotal evidence to show that the 'did you mean' spell checker follows the borrower usage pattern; the borrowing suggestions usage peaks one month after the peak in borrowing, perhaps indicating that users cannot locate the items they need as they are on loan, and so are using the suggestions option for related reading. The keyword tag-cloud clicks peak during October, again suggesting that new users are unsure of the content they require. In addition, the number of unique titles borrowed per calendar year rose significantly after borrower recommendations were soft-launched.

This is a largely print-based example; however, the implication for digital information is clear: these are the types of feature that are users are expecting from Google, Amazon, etc. The secret for libraries and resource-discovery vendors over the next five to ten years is how to go one stage further than the Huddersfield example, by using text and data mining to recommend both digital content at the user's fingertips and physical content, at the user's local library, in one place; how to move away from the traditional A&I database experience – 'your result returns zero hits' – by adding value, flexibility and personalization.

Personalization

Following on from highly successful usage-based recommendations by commercial services such as Amazon.com, ExLibris uses the bX recommender service, a collaboration of Ex Libris and the Los Alamos National Laboratory (LANL),[27] to provide recommendations based on usage data as an add-on service for customers. This move prompted the University of Huddersfield to start logging data from its SFX menu requests to see if there was potential in a similar in-house system. Although the test is at a very early stage, and will never be able to utilize the sheer amount of data generated by ExLibris, there is enough data to make recommendations at journal level.[28] The quality of these recommendations is now being tested.

Low usage or non-usage of resources is a perennial problem in libraries. However, the use of anonymized personal data may be of use in encouraging others to use systems; e.g. a first-year psychology student would be able to log in to the university portal to check e-mail, university virtual learning environment (VLE) etc.; the portal would also be able to recommend which books and journal articles to use for the course, based on previous undergraduates' experience, without the student ever needing to enter the library or use traditional methods of resource discovery. This may be seen as dumbing down or spoon-feeding; however, if it addresses the needs of the non-user by introducing resource discovery through recommendation or 'accidental discoveries', then there is benefit in such a system (King, 2008).

Privacy

Each time that your card is swiped, it registers not only the total amount spent, but exactly what you have spent it on. The supermarkets can therefore build up a customer profile of each card holder.

(Howell, 1995)

Is the cost of increased personalization an invasion of privacy? Surely, to understand users' needs we need to research them? In general, we do not object to using supermarket store cards, but these are not for our benefit, they are so that the store can see what we buy in order to better market its products to us.

A recent blog from Tony Hirst, 'Why Private Browsing Isn't . . .', discusses private browsing in the latest browsers, but then goes on to discuss how Flash's 'Stored Objects', an equivalent to cookies, sits outside private browsing and thus enables sites such as the BBC's iPlayer to resume a programme if you change browser (Hirst, 2009). Once again, the use of this data is not considered an invasion of privacy.

Jenny Walker suggests that librarians have been very cautious in this area: 'To date, user information-seeking behaviour data has been largely overlooked for enhancing library services, but steps are being taken in this direction, such as the development of recommender services and new metrics for scholarly evaluation' (Walker, 2009).

This chapter does not intend to tackle the finer points of data protection and ethics, but rather to make the point that the use of *anonymized* data is the real issue. It is only through the use of anonymized personal data that resource discovery can be improved/personalized in the ways described above. The only real concern is when a particular cohort is so small that usage can easily be mapped to individuals.

> Data Protection places significant demands on such an undertaking. Submitted records will not include individual user details and will be aggregated at the level of course/unit of study and item (e.g. book title). Furthermore, in the data used to derive activity patterns ('users who did this also did that'), lone transactions in a given group will also be removed.[29]

The JISC MOSAIC (Making Our Shared Activity Information Count) project plans to investigate the technical feasibility and issues around exploiting data to assist resource discovery and evaluation in higher education. Data is derived from:

- the circulation module of library management systems (the initial project focus)
- the ERM (environmental resources management) system/resolver journal article access
- VLE resource and learning object download
- reading lists (from a variety of institutional sources, without activity data), which may provide key indicators.

This work builds on the previous JISC TILE project[30] and the work of David Pattern at the University of Huddersfield,[31] who released over 80,000 titles derived from a pool of just under 3 million circulation transactions spanning a 13 year period, a major portion of book circulation and recommendation data, under an Open Data Commons licence.[32]

Pattern commented, 'This isn't about breaching borrower/patron privacy – the data we've released is thoroughly aggregated and anonymised. This is about sharing potentially useful data to a much wider community and attaching as few strings as possible.'

The vision for the next five to ten years

The impetus for change will come from students themselves as the behaviours and approaches apparent now become more deeply embedded in subsequent cohorts of entrants and the most positive of them – the experimentation, networking and collaboration, for example – are encouraged and reinforced through a school system seeking, in a reformed curriculum, to place greater emphasis on such dispositions.

(JISC, 2009)

The key for the medium term is to provide Google-like interfaces with Google-like results; there is a race to provide this through systems such as Summon, Primo and WorldCat Local, which will all use pre-harvested data rather than federated searching. WorldCat Local already provides social-networking tools.

Open source

This chapter has so far not touched on resource discovery via library management systems and next-generation catalogues in any detail, as it is anticipated that open-source library management systems such as Evergreen[33] and KOHA[34] and next-generation catalogue/library resource portals such as VuFind[35] will come to dominate the market over the next five to ten years. The implementation of open-source systems is gathering pace in the USA, and in Europe with the establishment of companies such as PTFS Europe;[36] and as previously missing modules such as Serials and Inter-Library Loans are soon to be released, these systems will soon become a reality. Some existing library management vendors, such as TALIS, already have an eye on the future with the Juice Project. Its aim is to make it easy to enhance library catalogues without duplication of effort, or, as Richard Wallis puts it, 'slap some mash on your OPAC' (Wallis, 2009a, 2009b).

Mash-ups

> The Mashup, where data from one or more sites is brought together to add value to the data on another site, is only four years old.[37]

The truth is, we will not know what the next Google will look like until it comes along – it will certainly include mash-ups with a whole lot more personalization and Web 2.0 functionality, such as blogs, personalized accounts, alerts, plug-ins and APIs, some of which may fall by the wayside as new features are developed (King, 2008; Nicholas et al. 2009).

We may even be in a situation where we can do it ourselves or use free stuff, e.g. Tony Hirst's work with Yahoo Pipes,[38] where he uses Scott Wilson's jOPML (Journals into OPML),[39] an application built using the data exported from the ticTOCS project[40] to:

- pull a list of journals in a particular subject area, based on user-provided keywords, into the Yahoo Pipes environment
- pull the most recent table of contents from those journals into that environment
- then filter those recent articles to display only the articles on a particular subtopic.

Ideally, harvested searches plugged into open-source library management systems/institutional repositories, etc., will become the preferred choice, allowing libraries to make sense of the anarchy by choosing separate, interoperable modules from a variety of existing suppliers, open-source communities and developers.

Visualization

> The main goal of *data visualization* is its ability to *visualize* data, communicating information clearly and effectively. It doesn't mean that data visualization needs to look boring to be functional or extremely sophisticated to look beautiful.   (*Smashing Magazine*, 2008)

Carol Tenopir (2007) asks '[is the] search box solution really the best for facilitating research?' The work of the Human-Computer Interaction Lab[41] and Edward Tufte,[42] amongst others, has led to data visualization gaining acceptance in recent years. Recently, Brendan Dawes (perform any search on his website to watch your results move across the pages as a number of insects[43]) created DoodleBuzz.com, a way to read the news through an experimental interface that allows you to create topographic maps of current news stories.[44] He was also commissioned by the BBC to re-design its Memoryshare website;[45] when this was shown at the recent Mashed Library 2009 event (Dawes, 2009) there was a palpable 'sharp intake of breath' from the librarians in the room at the replacement of a perfectly functional search box with a data visualisation page. This is an evolving area and will certainly be a part of the resource-discovery process in years to come. Certainly today, in its simplest form, it can transform a two-dimensional repository into a resource of obvious appeal to potential users, as the recent JISC-funded Kultur project shows,[46] or create a virtual bookshelf to reintroduce serendipity into library catalogue.[47]

What can't we afford not to do?

This chapter started by considering how A&I databases were being slashed in order to balance the budgets. However, there is also a cost in going to any new system, whether it is the new generation of harvested searches or the 'free beer, free kittens' approach that some see as being represented by the open-source systems (Pattern, 2009b).

Although the cost is there, can we afford to stay as we are? Two very different sessions at the 2009 UKSG Conference asked, 'Why is Google so easy and the library so hard?' (Duddy, 2009a) and 'Why do we want to teach our users to be librarians?' (Pattern, 2009a). They are important questions, and in themselves are justifications for investing in new systems, even in a period of financial hardship. With increasing attention being paid to National Student Surveys, resource discovery and e-resources provision can often be an open goal regarding negative student satisfaction.

> We're facing challenging budget years ahead. It's essential that we raise the profile of the library and demonstrate real value.   (Shipp, 2009)

New systems should allow us to avoid those duplications of A–Z lists on the web pages, the library catalogue and the link resolver, while bringing in isolated collections in other parts of the university, such as the repository, etc. What our users want is a Google search with Google-like results (Lauridsen and Stone, 2009). We must not make the mistake of assuming that Google and library resource-discovery systems are mutually exclusive, neither should we assume that just because Google is the first point of call it is the only one – one size does not fit all (King, 2008).

> Google indexes thousands of pages every day that are outside the realms of 'traditional' literature and academic discourse . . .
> . . . There is information out there that doesn't exist anywhere else.
> Google is a superb tool for locating it.   (Duddy, 2009b)

Our job over the next five to ten years is to provide a way to access these valuable resources in an intuitive, easy-to-use one-stop shop, and not to be afraid of running a continual beta test where new services and functions can be added as and when necessary. To do this we need flexible, interoperable resource-discovery systems based on open-source software. In addition, we must keep evaluating users' needs and reach out by adapting our systems to fit their requirements, rather than expecting them to come to us; indeed, our very future depends on it.

Notes

1 JISC Academic Database Assessment Tool (ADAT),
   www.jisc-adat.com/adat/home.pl [accessed 28 July 2009].

2 Research Excellence Framework,
   www.hefce.ac.uk/Research/ref/ [accessed 28 July 2009].

3 Summary of Latest Enhancements in Scopus,
   http://info.scopus.com/june_07/ [accessed 28 July 2009].

4 Thomson Reuters Links Article Match Retrieval,
   http://isiwebofknowledge.com/directlinks/amrfaq/ [accessed 28 July 2009].

5 Thomson Reuters to Participate in the Summon Service,
   www.serialssolutions.com/assets/attach_news/PR-Summon-WoS.pdf [accessed
   28 July 2009].

6 JISC Digitisation Programme,
   www.jisc.ac.uk/digitisation [accessed 28 July 2009].

7 JISC Digitisation Programme, Digi Posters: at-a-glance guide to all the
   digitisation projects:
   www.jisc.ac.uk/media/documents/programmes/digitisation/digiposters.pdf
   [accessed 28 July 2009].

8 JISC Enriching Digital Resources,
   www.jisc.ac.uk/whatwedo/programmes/digitisation/enrichingdigi.aspx [accessed
   28 July 2009].

9 Data Audit Framework,
   www.data-audit.eu/ [accessed 28 July 2009].

10 JISC Standards Catalogue,
    http://standards-catalogue.ukoln.ac.uk/index/Standards_Entries [accessed 28
    July 2009].

11 DOI System Overview: introduction,
    www.doi.org/overview/sys_overview_021601.html [accessed 28 July 2009].

12 CrossRef,
    www.crossref.org/ [accessed 28 July 2009].

13 Research Assessment Exercise,
    www.rae.ac.uk/ [accessed 28 July 2009].

14 UKSG,
    www.uksg.org/ [accessed 28 July 2009].

15 FRBRization in the Open Library,
    http://openlibrary.org/about/frbrization [accessed 28 July 2009].

16 KBART: Knowledge Bases And Related Tools Working Group,
    www.uksg.org/kbart [accessed 28 July 2009].

17 KBART Monitoring Group Report, February 2009,
www.uksg.org/sites/uksg.org/files/kbart_monitors_report_feb09.pdf [accessed
28 July 2009].

18 WebFeat: a brief history,
www.webfeat.org/about.htm [accessed 28 July 2009].

19 Web Services Librarian,
http://webserviceslibrarian.blogspot.com/ [accessed 28 July 2009].

20 Summon:
www.serialssolutions.com/summon/ [accessed 28 July 2009].

21 Primo:
www.exlibrisgroup.com/category/PrimoOverview [accessed 28 July 2009].

22 Worldcat Local:
www.oclc.org/worldcatlocal/ [accessed 28 July 2009].

23 LexisNexis Signs on to the Summon Service,
www.serialssolutions.com/assets/attach_news/PR-Summon-LexisNexis.pdf
[accessed 28 July 2009].

24 xISBN,
www.oclc.org/research/projects/xisbn [accessed 28 July 2009].

25 LibraryThing APIs,
www.librarything.com/api [accessed 28 July 2009].

26 University of Huddersfield, Applied Economics Letters, Table of Contents and
Recent Articles:
http://library.hud.ac.uk/catlink/bib/592251/cls/ [accessed 28 July 2009].

27 bX Recommender Service: overview,
www.exlibrisgroup.com/category/bXOverview [accessed 28 July 2009].

28 University of Huddersfield, British Journal of Midwifery, people who looked at
this journal also looked at these journals,
http://library.hud.ac.uk/catlink/bib/241308/cls/ [accessed 28 August 2009].

29 JISC MOSAIC,
www.sero.co.uk/jisc-mosaic.html [accessed 28 July 2009].

30 Towards Implementation of Library 2.0 and the e-Framework (TILE),
www.jisc.ac.uk/whatwedo/programmes/resourcediscovery/tile.aspx [accessed 28
July 2009].

31 Pattern, D., Free Book Usage Data from the University of Huddersfield,
www.daveyp.com/blog/archives/528 [accessed 28 July 2009].

32 Open Data Commons,
www.opendatacommons.org/ [accessed 28 July 2009].

33 Evergreen,
www.open-ils.org/ [accessed 28 July 2009].

34 KOHA,
http://koha.org/ [accessed 28 July 2009].

35 VuFind:
www.vufind.org/ [accessed 28 July 2009].

36 PTFS Europe,
www.ptfs-europe.com/ [accessed 28 July 2009].

37 The Library 2.0 Gang,
http://librarygang.talis.com/ [accessed 28 July 2009].

38 Mashlib Pipes Tutorial: 2D journal search,
http://ouseful.wordpress.com/2009/07/09/mashlib-pipes-tutorial-2d-journal-search/ [accessed 28 July 2009].

39 Scott Wilson, jOPML,
http://jopml.org/ [accessed 28 July 2009].

40 TicTocs: journal tables of contents service, www.tictocs.ac.uk/ [accessed 28 July 2009].

41 University of Maryland Institute for Advanced Computer Studies, Human-Computer Interaction Lab,
www.cs.umd.edu/hcil/ [accessed 28 July 2009].

42 The Work of Edward Tufte and Graphics Press,
www.edwardtufte.com/tufte/ [accessed 28 July 2009].

43 brendandawes.com,
www.brendandawes.com/ [accessed 28 July 2009].

44 DoodleBuzz, Typographic News Explore,
www.doodlebuzz.com/ [accessed 28 July 2009].

45 BBC Memoryshare,
www.bbc.co.uk/dna/memoryshare/ [accessed 28 July 2009].

46 UAL Research Online,
http://kultur.arts.ac.uk [accessed 28 July 2009].

47 University of Huddersfield, 1960s Fashion Print: a sourcebook,
http://library.hud.ac.uk/catlink/bib/614544/cls/ [accessed 28 July 2009].

References

Apps, A. and MacIntyre, R. (2006) Why OpenURL?, *D-Lib Magazine*, 12 (5). DOI: 10.1045/may2006-apps.

Beit-Arie, O., Blake, M., Caplan, P., Flecker, D., Ingoldsby, T., Lannom, L. W., Mischo, W. H., Pentz, E., Rogers, S. and Van de Sompel, H. (2001) Linking to the Appropriate Copy, *D-Lib Magazine*, 7 (9). DOI: 10.1045/september2001-caplan.

Berners Lee, T. (1998) *Cool URIs Don't Change*, www.w3.org/Provider/Style/URI [accessed 28 July 2009].

Cameron, R. D. (1997) *A Universal Citation Database as a Catalyst for Reform in Scholarly Communication*, http://elib.cs.sfu.ca/project/papers/citebase/citebase.html [accessed 28 July 2009].

Canós Cerdá, J. H., Nieto, E. M. and Campos, M. L. (2009) What's Wrong with Citation Counts?, *D-Lib Magazine*, 15 (3/4). DOI: 10.1045/march2009-canos.

CIBER (2007), *Information Behaviour of the Researcher of the Future* ('Google Generation' Project), University College London, CIBER, www.ucl.ac.uk/infostudies/research/ciber/downloads/ggexecutive.pdf [accessed 28 July 2009].

CIBER (2009) *E-journals: their, use, value and impact, a CIBER Report for the Research Information Network*, www.ucl.ac.uk/infostudies/research/ciber/RINjournals.pdf [accessed 5 November 2009].

Corbyn, Z. (2009) Expect Few New Titles in Library as Sterling's Fall Pounds Acquisitions, *Times Higher Education*, 21 May, www.timeshighereducation.co.uk/story.asp?storycode=406612 [accessed 28 July 2009].

Culling, J. (2007) *Link Resolvers and the Serials Supply Chain: final project report for UKSG*, Oxford, Scholarly Information Strategies, www.uksg.org/sites/uksg.org/files/uksg_link_resolvers_final_report.pdf [accessed 28 July 2009].

Dawes, B. (2009) *Somewhere I Have Never Travelled*, Mash Oop North, University of Huddersfield, 7 July, www.archive.org/details/MashOopNorth_BrendanDawes/ [accessed 28 July 2009].

Duddy, C. (2009a) *A Student Perspective on Accessing Academic Information in the Google Era*, 32nd UKSG Annual Conference and Exhibition, 30 March–1 April, Riviera International Conference Centre, Torquay.

Duddy, C. (2009b) A Personal Perspective on Accessing Academic Information in the Google Era, or 'How I learned to stop worrying and love Google', *Serials*, 22 (2), 132–5. DOI: 10.1629/22131.

Gibson, I., Goddard, L. and Gordon, S. (2009) One Box to Search Them All: implementing federated search at an academic library, *Library Hi Tech*, **27** (1), 118–33. DOI 10.1108/07378830910942973.

HCSTC (UK House of Commons Science and Technology Committee) (2004) *Scientific Publications: free for all?* Tenth report of session 2003–04, House of Commons papers 2003–04, 399-II, www.publications.parliament.uk/pa/cm200304/cmselect/cmsctech/399/ 39902.htm [accessed 28 July 2009].

Helfer, D. and Wakimoto, J. (2007) *Federated Search: the good, the bad and the ugly*, Special Libraries Association Annual Conference, 4–6 June, Denver, Colorado, www.slideshare.net/dorishelfer/federated-search-the-good-the-bad-and-the-ugly [accessed 28 July 2009].

Hirst, T. (2009) *Why Private Browsing Isn't . . . ,* http://ouseful.wordpress.com/2009/07/15/why-private-browsing-isnt/ [accessed 28 July 2009].

Howell, F. (1995) What Price Customer Loyalty? Supermarket shoppers will get discounts under glitzy new schemes. But Big Brother may come to rule the till, *Independent*, 21 October, www.independent.co.uk/money/what-price-customer-loyalty-supermarket-shoppers-will-get-discounts-under-glitzy-new-schemes-but-big-brother-may-come-to-rule-the-till-1578705.html [accessed 28 July 2009].

JISC (2009) *Higher Education in a Web 2.0 World: report of an independent Committee of Inquiry into the impact on higher education of students' widespread use of Web 2.0 technologies*, JISC, www.jisc.ac.uk/publications/documents/heweb2.aspx [accessed 28 July 2009].

King, D. (2008) Many Libraries Have Gone to Federated Searching to Win Users Back From Google: is it working? *Journal of Electronic Resources Librarianship*, **20** (4), 213–27. DOI: 10.1080/19411260802554520.

Lampert, L. D. and Dabbour, K. S. (2007) Librarian Perspectives on Teaching Metasearch and Federated Search Technologies, *Internet Reference Services Quarterly*, **12** (3/4), 253–78. DOI: 10.1300/J136v12n03_02.

Lauridsen, H. and Stone, G. (2009) The 21st-century Library: a whole new ball game? *Serials*, **22** (2), 141–5. DOI: 10.1629/22141.

Lederman, S. (2008) *Federated Search Roadmap: Part II – identifying benefits*, http://federatedsearchblog.com/2008/06/30/federated-search-roadmap-part-ii-identifying-benefits/ [accessed 28 July 2009].

Lederman, S. (2009) *Beyond Federated Search?*,
http://federatedsearchblog.com/2009/03/19/beyond-federated-search/#
more-241 [accessed 28 July 2009].

Meyer, C. A. (2008), Reference Accuracy: best practices for making the links,
Journal of Electronic Publishing, 11 (2). DOI: 10.3998/3336451.0011.206.

Nicholas, D. (2008) If We Do Not Understand Our Users, We Will Certainly Fail.
In Stone, G., Anderson, R. and Feinstein, J. (eds), *E-Resources Management
Handbook*, Oxford, UKSG. DOI: 10.1629/9552448_0_3.13.1.

Nicholas, D., Huntington, P., Jamali, H. R., Rowlands, I. and Fieldhouse, M. (2009)
Student Digital Information-seeking Behaviour in Context, *Journal of
Documentation*, 65 (1), 106–32. DOI: 10.1108/00220410910926149.

NISO (National Information Standards Organization) (2004) The OpenURL
Framework for Context-sensitive Services,
www.techstreet.com/cgi-bin/detail?product_id=1262106ANSI/
NISO Z39.88-2004 – *The OpenURL Framework for Context-Sensitive Services*
[accessed 28 July 2009].

Nygren, E., Haya, G. and Widmark, W. (2006) *Students Experience of Metalib and
Google Scholar*, Stockholm, Universitetsbiblioteket,
http://urn.kb.se/resolve?urn=urn:nbn:se:su:diva-1264 [accessed 28 July 2009].

Pattern, D. (2009a) *OPAC 2.0 and Beyond*, 32nd UKSG Annual Conference and
Exhibition, 30 March–1 April, Riviera International Conference Centre,
Torquay,
http://eprints.hud.ac.uk/4143/ [accessed 28 July 2009].

Pattern, D. (2009b) *Did Someone Ssay 'Free Beer'?!* In Open Source: 'Free Speech, Free
Beer and Free Kittens!', University of Huddersfield, 26 June,
http://eprints.hud.ac.uk/4850/ [accessed 28 July 2009].

RIN (Research Information Network) (2006) *Researchers and Discovery Services:
behaviour, perceptions and needs,* a study commissioned by the Research
Information Network,
www.rin.ac.uk/researchers-discovery-services [accessed 28 July 2009].

RIN (Research Information Network) (2008) *Ensuring a Bright Future for Research
Libraries: A guide for vice-chancellors and senior institutional managers*,
www.rin.ac.uk/files/Ensuring_bright_future_guide_Nov08@.pdf [accessed 28
July 2009].

Rochkind, J. (2009) Beyond Federated Search? Comments,
http://federatedsearchblog.com/2009/03/19/beyond-federated-search/
#comments [accessed 28 July 2009].

Shipp, J. (2009) University Librarian at the University of Sydney, comment at the Sydney Online conference, January.

Smashing Magazine (2008) Editorial: Data visualization and infographics, *Smashing Magazine*, 14 January, www.smashingmagazine.com/2008/01/14/monday-inspiration-data-visualization-and-infographics/ [accessed 28 July 2009].

Tenopir, C. (2007) Online Databases: can Johnny search?, *Library Journal*, 132 (2), 30, www.libraryjournal.com/article/CA6407784.html?industryid=47130 [accessed 28 July 2009].

Tonkin, E. (2008) Persistent Identifiers: considering the options, *Ariadne*, 56, www.ariadne.ac.uk/issue56/tonkin/ [accessed 28 July 2009].

UKRDS (UK Research Data Service) (2008) *The UK Research Data Service Feasibility Study,* report and recommendations to HEFCE, 19 December, www.ukrds.ac.uk/HEFCE%20UKRDS%20Final%20Report%20V%201.1.doc [accessed 28 July 2009].

Van de Sompel, H., Hochstenbach, P. and Beit-Arie, O. (2000) OpenURL Syntax Description, draft version 0.1, www.openurl.info/registry/docs/pdf/openurl-01.pdf [accessed 28 July 2009].

Walker, D. (2007) Building Custom Metasearch Interfaces and Services Using the MetaLib X-server, *Internet Reference Services Quarterly*, 12 (3/4), 325–39. DOI: 10.1300/J136v12n03_06.

Walker, J. (2009) Key Issue: mining information-seeking behaviour data to enhance library services, *Serials*, 22 (2), 182–4. DOI: 10.1629/22182.

Wallis, R. (2009a) Juice Up Your OPAC, *Panlibus*, 12, 12–13.

Wallis, R. (2009b) *Juice Project*, Mash Oop North, University of Huddersfield, 7 July, http://mashlib09.wordpress.com/ [accessed 28 July 2009].

7

Who owns the content in the digital environment?

Wilma Mossink and Lorraine Estelle

Introduction

> Libraries have two roles essential to the IP balance: archiving the
> national memory and allowing the public and research community access
> to it. [1]

Any book dealing with the future of digital information would be incomplete without considering the issues of intellectual property (IP). Although the internet casts a new light on these issues, the principal problems are not new. In the 19th century the American publishing industry was quick to recognize that in sharing a language with the UK, it was easy to share its literature too. English texts were open to piracy, and it was easier and more profitable to appropriate an English text than to pay an American author. This had a depressing effect on the US publishing industry, and for decades American authors expressed their frustration at being underpaid because of the availability of cheap pirated copies of UK publications. Equally, renowned British authors such as Charles Dickens were paid nothing for the many thousands of copies of their books sold in the USA. Indeed, Dickens, while on a reading tour of the USA, made many pleas for international copyright laws. His fans, enjoying access to cheap copies of his books, were not impressed; for example, they paid the equivalent of 6 cents per copy for a book such as *A Christmas Carol*, which cost $2.50 in the UK (Vaidhyanathan, 2001). It was not until the 1890s that international copyright agreements began to resolve the situation.

Arguably, since the late 19th century copyright law has evolved to protect the intellectual property of authors and creators, to cultivate a vibrant creative arts industry, and to allow for fair dealing on the part of the buying or reading public. Fair dealing is the 'right' to make a copy from an in-copyright work without permission from or payment to the rights holder, if that copy is for non-commercial research or educational purposes. The only requirement is to acknowledge the source of the copied work. Most individual copying by researchers at universities for academic purposes is done under the fair dealing provisions.

However, the evolution of copyright law took place in an analogue world and so it has not really adapted to the digital world. This leaves room either for too much order or, as many would argue in the light of the recent developments in the music industry, a state of copyright anarchy.

The digital world provides opportunities never before envisaged for the sharing, repurposing and reusing of content. Distribution of content is relatively cheap, and does not require the infrastructure needed for traditional publishing. This situation has created a great tension between the publishing industry and the academic sector. Authors can easily distribute their works; academics can take content from various sources and create new works that provide innovations in research or teaching, and of course users can effortlessly share content with their friends or colleagues. How can we use new technologies to their maximum potential for informal distribution and creative use and reuse of content while at the same time preserving the traditional publishing model?

The question is a complex one, and all types of content and all areas of the publishing sector are affected. For example, a mash-up combines data from two or more external sources to create a new dataset. The new result creates a distinct application that was not the reason for producing the raw source data. A good example is A Vision of Britain, a website that provides a unique and comprehensive history of the country. The website was created by putting together (or mashing up) maps, photographs, census data, statistical data and travel writing. The production of such a resource is extremely innovative, but it can also be a copyright nightmare. All the authors or owners of the original source material need to be found and their permissions sought in order to publish the newly derived dataset, and this is a costly and onerous process. If one of the original data or content owners refuses permission (and they may well), the entire mash-up cannot be published on the internet.

The use of software robots that crawl the internet to collect scientific information, which is then aggregated and processed to arrive at new insights, or even to create new knowledge, presents another problem. A good example is the work of Peter Murray-Rust, who 'spent six months going through the [chemistry] literature and came home with several hundred datapoints. Each datapoint was the product of a visit to the library to find a single piece of information in a journal.' Murray-Rust realized that a great many discoveries rely on using the information in literature, but this requires an (exceptional) human being to digest a huge mass of seemingly unrelated data. After creating software robots to undertake this task, Murray-Rust was able to do in minutes what had taken months in the library. For this method of data mining to work, publishers must allow the robots into their servers to crawl the literature. Some publishers are reluctant to do so, arguing that they own everything in an article they publish: the text and the embedded data. Arguably the 'facts' extracted are not subject to copyright, but nonetheless a lack of clarity in copyright law can inhibit the publication and sharing of this new 'aggregated' knowledge. This problem applies not only to chemistry but also to many sorts of intellectual property, such as map data, climate data, traffic data and historic texts (Pounder, 2008).

Publishers of digital material who are concerned with protecting their intellectual property have two methods at their disposal. The first of these is the licence agreement; this is a contract between the library and the publisher setting out how the content in an electronic resource can be used and what the restrictions are. Usually such licences permit fair use, and in some cases grant the user even more than is required in copyright law. In other instances, publishers' licences can seek to restrict use beyond what is considered fair in the print world. The issue of contracts undermining copyright law is an area of tension, and one where the academic sector and the publishing industry (and probably legislators) need to find consensus.

The second method is the use of the digital rights management (DRM): technological tools used to regulate the access and use of digital data. These tools are designed to prohibit copyright infringements and to prevent digital piracy. For example, DRM systems may enable a user to see the content on a publisher's server, but restrict other activity that the user may want to undertake, such as the systematic downloading of a whole journal or an entire database of content. Some systems will also recognize and 'lock-out' software robots or human users who download too much content too quickly. Unfortunately, some DRM systems also prevent users undertaking activity which is lawful and considered in the print world to be fair use, such as the copying of limited amounts of text for academic use.

Another problem for the academic sector is that fair dealing does not apply to multimedia resources such as film and sound records or podcasts. In certain academic disciplines this is a very serious restriction, and means that it is impossible (without seeking permission) for the researcher to include short clips of sound or film recording (or even still images) in academic works or in teaching materials. In the UK, the Gowers Review of Intellectual Property (HM Treasury, 2006) recommended that film and sound recordings should be included in fair dealing, but so far there has not been legislation to implement this.

In 2008 the British Library (2008) carried out a survey of intellectual property and argued that 'Digital is not Different'. In the survey, 93% of respondents agreed that anyone involved in non-commercial research should be allowed to copy parts of electronically published works such as journal articles, news broadcasts and film or sound recordings. As a result, the library sector has strongly advocated that copyright exceptions (fair dealing) should apply to all types of content (including audiovisual material), whether published in print or in digital form.

Orphan works are another area of concern for the academic sector. The term 'orphan work' refers to any content (text, image, film or sound, etc.) that belongs to an unknown person or organization. Chapter 5 describes the benefits to research, and indeed to the general public, of the mass digitization of historic resources. However, copyright law (in the EU) gives a copyright term of the life of the author plus 70 years. This means that anyone managing a project to digitize historical content, whether conducted by a publisher or by the academic sector, must spend many (costly) hours in locating and seeking permission of the authors of so called 'orphan works'. Currently, digitization projects are much more costly and time consuming than they need be, precisely because of the effort required to track down and find the IP owners. In its response to the Gowers Review, the British Library called for a 'light touch' system that would protect such projects from litigation, provided that a reasonable amount of attention was given to finding the owners of orphan works.

Finding the balance between the need to prevent copyright theft and the non-commercial needs of the academic sector is not easy. With justification, many publishers are concerned about copyright infringements, in particular, digital piracy. Websites such as Pirate Bay, Minova.org, isoHunt.com and Torrent Reactor allow users to search for and download BitTorrent files (torrents), small files that contain metadata necessary to download data files from other users. Other pirate sites make a wide range of e-books available for illegal download, although publishers may take comfort in the reported fact that the out-of-copyright *Kamasutra* tops the list of the ten most downloaded books on BitTorrent in 2009.[2] To highlight the extent of a the problem, the following is an extract from a discussion on an open web forum:

> Is there any site from where I can download free ebooks? I don't want public domain and classic ones. I want bestsellers and really exciting ones.

> If you download uTorrent, you can download books to it from mininova.org all in about a minute. I did that yesterday because I couldn't find my freaking book.[3]

A final and unique issue concerns the sharing of academic research. In scholarly publishing, the author of an academic article does not seek remuneration from the publisher, but rather recognition. The researcher freely gives his or her work to the publisher, and thus it might be argued that the researchers should also be free to share their (often publicly funded) work with their peers for scholarly purposes. Some journal publishers, on the other hand, would argue that the editorial and peer-review services that they provide cannot be sustained if authors freely share their content on the open web. Some publishers seek to prohibit authors completely from disseminating the peer-reviewed article and demand exclusive rights, while other publishers allow the authors to disseminate their work through their own websites or institutional repositories, usually after an embargo period of around six months.

The issues are complex and rarely black and white. For some years, the academic community has been engaged in a number of initiatives and projects which aim to bring clarity to the IP concerns outlined above. The rest of this chapter describes the work which the academic sector in Europe has undertaken to address the issues that currently restrict its ability to innovate.

Academic writing and the copyright arrangement

The fact that this book covers the ownership of digital content points to the lack of clarity on this matter. For a long time this lack of clarity has also been a problem within the world of higher education. The rise and development of digital libraries started an extensive discussion about ownership of scientific publications. It has been going on for a long time, and its significance within the debate on accessibility and dissemination of scientific information seems to be undiminished, although it now receives less attention. Whether this is due to exhaustion of interest or to the availability of clear answers remains to be seen. It is noticeable, however, that the debate, instead of focusing on the question of ownership, has shifted towards how to make scientific information available.

That questions had arisen about ownership of scientific information in the first place resulted from an important policy in institutions of higher education: the creation of a substantial digital library that permits searching of and access to full-text materials. Lack of clarity regarding ownership of the papers to be included in the digital library was an impediment to its development and expansion. Whether ownership of a scholarly text vests in the creator, the institution employing the creator, or the publisher of the text, has a great bearing on the chances of that publication's being included in the library.

Towards the end of the 1990s and around the early 2000s, various studies (ETUS, undated; McSherry, 2001; Monotti and Ricketson, 2003; Wiseman, 1999; C) were performed and policy recommendations were written (Intellectual Property Task Force, 1999; Mossink, 1999; Weedon, 2000; Weedon and Mossink, 2006) to give direction to the debate about ownership of scientific publications. Since then, the topic seems to have remained dormant, with hardly any new articles becoming available on it. The impact of these studies and the resulting policy recommendations are difficult to assess, but it is worth investigating whether detailed rules made by institutions of higher education have provided a stimulus for improving the accessibility of scholarly output, or whether, instead, a practice without detailed institutional regulations leads to more positive results.

This chapter addresses digital scholarly output. In the scholarly environment three declarations on Open Access are considered to be guiding. The best known, the Berlin Declaration (Max Planck Gesellschaft, 2003), lists the types of scholarly work protected by copyright and covered by the Declaration: 'Open access contributions include original scientific research results, raw data and metadata, source materials, digital representations of pictorial and graphical materials and scholarly multimedia material.'

To answer the question 'Who owns digital content?' we will concentrate on research output, and specifically on journal articles. These are by far the main focus both of policy documents from institutions of higher education and of interest from the scientific community. Although they are, by and large, subject to the same regime of intellectual property and rules of first ownership, the interpretation of the law by institutions of higher education differs greatly between different scholarly outputs. For example, scholarly multimedia materials in general are often considered to be educational rather than research output, and they are hardly ever included and discussed in institutional copyright policies; the policy of the SURF Foundation, which also includes works other than journal articles, is an exception. Raw data are mentioned more often, and it is to be expected that, because of new developments regarding the reuse of data and underlying sources, these copyright policies will be subject to change.

Although the legal provisions pertaining to the ownership of works made in the course of employment are unambiguous, their interpretation by universities, and the established practices of universities, have confused the debate. When universities waive their copyright (see below), the academic staff act as copyright owners in their relationships with publishers, and publishers act as if academic staff have the legal right to assign copyright (Law, Weedon and Sheen, 2000).

It has become apparent that the established practices for reaching agreement on ownership of scientific publications are difficult to manage. Several players are involved – authors, libraries, institutions, publishers and the public – each with their own interests, and these interests have to be balanced so as to safeguard optimal access to information. One way of achieving this is by establishing a copyright arrangement in which the bundle of rights stemming from copyright law is distributed in such a manner that each player gets the latitude they need for the expression of their interests or activities.

The Zwolle Principles

This search for balance has led to the Zwolle Principles, a set of core principles focused on the thoughtful understanding and application of copyright law to the management of scholarly works, which can stimulate the principal stakeholders in scholarly communication to achieve maximum access to scholarship, to strengthen academic freedom and to enhance the quality of academic work (SURF Foundation, 2006).

The Zwolle Principles resulted from the three Zwolle conferences, dedicated to copyright management in higher education (the name Zwolle derives from the place where the conferences were held, a medieval town in the Netherlands). Reaching a copyright arrangement between the principal stakeholders was the chief aim of these conferences (Harvey, 2003; Crews and van Westrienen, 2007), the last of which took place early in 2004. Its aim was to achieve beneficial changes in copyright management issues by actually implementing the Zwolle Principles, which had already been accepted.

Current copyright positions and the future implications for scholars

The author's position
UK law

In the UK, legally, the author or creator is the first owner of copyright in a literary, dramatic, musical or artistic work.[4] However, if such a work is made by an employee in the course of employment, the employer is the first owner, unless a contractual arrangement stipulates differently. According to this provision, a university is the copyright owner of scholarly output. Nevertheless, universities have never assumed the position of ownership. In practice, they have waived their rights and still do so; they hardly ever formally claim their copyright. Thus, custom and practice have established the position that, in higher education in the UK, copyright in scholarly works generally lies with employees. A JISC (Joint Information Systems Committee) study conducted in 2000 showed that a majority of those universities that had a copyright policy had waived their copyright in journal articles and books (Weedon, 2000). A 2005 study on copyright policies in the Netherlands and the UK came to the same conclusion (Weedon and Mossink, 2006).

Exceptions to the established practice of university scholars owning copyright in their works are where institutions commission a piece of work specifically from a member of staff, or where the work is funded by an external organization. Here, copyright may be assigned to the institution or the funding organization as part of the agreement or contract.

USA law

If a work fulfils the requirements for protection, ownership of copyright will, in principle, be assigned to the maker.[5] However, the USA Copyright Act, like that of the UK, contains a clause allowing for someone other than the maker to be the legal owner of the copyright; this is the 'work made for hire doctrine'. According to this doctrine, an employer or a commissioning party (who pays for the creation of the work) is deemed to be the author, rather than the employee or commissioned party (who actually conceives and fixes the expression).[6] There are two categories of work made for hire: works made by employees, and works made on commission. Different rules apply to the two categories.

The first category is a work prepared in the course of employment. The courts in the USA take a number of factors into consideration when deciding whether a work falls into this category: whether it is of the kind that an employee was employed to prepare, whether its preparation takes place primarily within the employer's time and place specifications, and whether the work was initiated, at least in part, by a purpose to serve the employer. Other factors may be considered, such as an employer's having the right to direct and supervise the way which the employee carries out his work, the means used for this and the method by which the employee is paid. The second category of a work made for hire is that done by an independent contractor. In theory, the 'work made for hire doctrine' means that a university owns the copyright of works made by its staff. The US courts, however, have created a 'teacher exception' to the work made for hire doctrine, allowing academics to own copyright in their works.[7]

Notwithstanding the copyright law provisions on ownership in the USA, universities do take different views concerning the appropriate balance of interests between universities and their academics with respect to their work (Crews and Wong, 2004).

The scholars' viewpoint

The creators of the information, the scholars, play a pivotal role in the debate on ownership and in the dissemination of scientific information, but their voice is not often heard and their opinion is mostly voiced by librarians and repository managers. They are sometimes approached to discover their wishes but, on the whole, they are difficult to reach and they tend not to look after their rights because they are not very interested in them (Davenport, 1994). Copyright is viewed as a difficult issue with many exceptions and detailed regulations, and copyright policies tend not to raise much enthusiasm and response – even when they aim at wider distribution of scholarly output. When authors are indeed involved in the drawing up of policy, much is made of this fact (Crawford, 2008; Suber, 2008).

By interviewing scholars directly, their preferences can be ascertained (Morris, 2009). Copyright is not a primary concern for them; they are interested in the dissemination of their works mainly by sending copies to others outside their institutions and by incorporating them into other works.

In the copyright arrangement, the position of authors appears to be largely established; it seems to be generally accepted that the scholarly author retains the rights to his publications. Nonetheless, the growth of the Open Access (OA) movement and the increase in the number of institutional repositories has led to shifts in authors' position within the copyright arrangement, due to the mandates formulated by several institutions (EPrints, 2009). Authors are being either encouraged or obliged to publish their scholarly output in OA journals, or to deposit post-prints of their articles in their institution's digital repository.

The position of institutions

It is not just the authors who show little interest in the management of their rights; for institutions, also, copyright has been an unpopular issue until recently. In 2006 the SURF Foundation and JISC published a survey of established practices regarding copyright in institutions of higher education in the Netherlands and the UK. The study showed that only a few universities had formal policies relating to intellectual property ownership in the journal articles produced by their academic and research staff (Weedon and Mossink, 2006). If they had a copyright policy at all, it tended to focus mainly on the use of material produced by the institution itself, specifying principles of fair use, the use of works in course packs and interlibrary loan.

Since the rise of digital libraries and the establishment of institutional repositories, the focus in copyright policies has shifted to the question of ownership – and incidentally, this did not immediately cause more institutions to establish policies. However, it is noticeable that institutions are now both demanding and claiming a more important position within the copyright arrangement, mainly as a result of the spread of OA ideals and the concomitant growth of institutional repositories.

The Berlin Declaration

In addition to OA journals, institutions of higher education increasingly consider repositories to be the right method for disseminating scholarly output. Inspired by the Berlin Declaration, many institutions have joined a worldwide network of repositories. The Berlin Declaration, in its succinctness, points towards the essence of the internet and its importance for digital information: a medium that guarantees worldwide access and global and interactive use of scholarly information and cultural heritage. The 264 signatories to the Declaration acknowledge this and state that they 'feel obliged to address the challenges of the Internet as an emerging functional medium for distributing knowledge' (Max Planck Gesellschaft, 2009). They support the transition to the electronic OA paradigm by distributing works as OA publications and, in compliance with the requirements of the Berlin Declaration, by depositing a 'complete version of the work and all supplemental materials in at least one online repository that is supported and maintained by a well-established organization that seeks to enable Open Access, unrestricted distribution, interoperability, and long term archiving'. Furthermore, they want to express through a licence that all users are allowed to copy, use, distribute, transmit and display the work publicly and to make and distribute derivative works, in any digital medium for any responsible purpose, subject to proper attribution of authorship. Users have the right to make small numbers of printed copies for their personal use (Max Planck Gesellschaft, 2003).

DAREnet

In filling their repositories, institutions were once again faced with a copyright problem, as they had been when starting their digital libraries. The transfer of copyright by the authors to the publishers as quid pro quo for getting their works published now obstructed the addition of those works to a repository and their subsequent accessibility to a third party. To give their repositories substance, some institutions chose not so much to develop policies as to start practical initiatives, like the 'hunDAREdthousand' programme, which was introduced in the Netherlands.

Under this programme, a large Digital Academic Repositories (DARE) project under the name 'honDAREdduizend' started on 1 October 2005, in which all Dutch universities, the Netherlands Organisation for Scientific Research (NWO) and the Royal Netherlands Academy of Art and Sciences (KNAW) sought to increase the number of full-text publications in the repositories to 100,000 within one year. This programme built on the SURF Foundation's DAREnet portal to the localized digital archives of all Dutch universities and some affiliated institutions. DAREnet has now been taken over by KNAW and is integrated with the scientific portal NARCIS.

The DAREnet subsets 'Keur der Wetenschap' (Cream of Science), containing publications of leading Dutch researchers, and 'Nationale proefschriftensite' (National PhD Thesis Site) have become especially well known. The collections, during their compilation, caused both the biggest and the smallest of problems. Resolution of the biggest problem – getting permission from the copyright owner (usually the publisher) to include the work in and make it accessible through the repository – was greatly facilitated by three factors: the output of only a relatively small group of scholars was concerned, in several cases copyright was still owned by the authors and, in addition, the publishers were favourably disposed towards the project.

The scholarly output that has been stored in repositories so far consists mainly of articles published in scientific journals. This may change in the future because of the increasing addition of research data. In virtually all cases, the rights to the articles have been transferred to publishers.

The RoMEO project

Requesting and acquiring permission from copyright owners for every article is a time-consuming process. In the UK, this has led to a different practical approach: the RoMEO project (Rights MEtadata for Open archiving). This project investigated the rights issues surrounding the self-archiving of research in the UK scholarly community. By surveying the academic community it ascertained how research literature and metadata was used and how it should be protected. From this work, the RoMEO project created a list of publishers' conditions for self-archiving. The RoMEO project is now part of SHERPA (Securing a Hybrid Environment for Research Preservation and Access) and is a point of reference for the copyright policies of English-language scientific journals, in particular, with a few national additions (SHERPA, 2006). The SHERPA/RoMEO service lists publishers' copyright conditions regarding authors archiving their work online, categorizing publishers and their conditions into four classes, using the colours green, blue, yellow and white to indicate the permissions that are normally given as part of each publisher's copyright transfer agreement. Each publisher's default policy on the author's right of self-archiving is listed.

Protecting intellectual property while enabling the widest possible use

A less time-consuming and possibly less costly approach than acquiring permission from the copyright owner might be to establish a clear strategy on copyright ownership and copyright management, with explicit provisions on how authors should proceed to safeguard public accessibility of publicly financed collective output. Authors need to be made aware and informed of the consequences of copyright ownership and transfer. They should realize that they need to preserve important rights. An institution could achieve this by decreeing that authors should retain their rights in their relationships with publishers, either by means of an author addendum or by making a licence that facilitates wider distribution of their articles. An increasing number of institutions have recently decreed such measures.

Licence to Publish

In order to establish balanced copyright management and provide improved access to scholarly information, JISC and SURF have developed the 'Copyright Toolkit' (SURF Foundation, undated). An important part of the Copyright Toolkit is the 'Licence to Publish'. When publishing under this licence in subscription-based journals, authors do not transfer their copyright to the publisher, but retain it for themselves. This allows authors to deposit their work in an institutional repository or subject repository, and to distribute it further as an OA contribution. The Licence to Publish has been created as a uniform licence that can be accepted as a standard by universities, authors and publishers. To make it acceptable, its preamble explicitly states that author and publisher believe that it is in the general interest to grant maximum access to scholarly and/or scientific works without compromising quality or academic freedom, especially when public resources finance such works, and that a balance should be established between author and publisher so as to achieve this.

Underlying the Licence to Publish are several principles that express the balance between author and publisher in the copyright arrangement. These include retention of rights by the author and permission for the publisher to reproduce and distribute the work, and an optional embargo period before publication, allowing for financial compensation for publication of the work. Under the licence, the article will be published on a publicly accessible institutional and/or subject repository immediately after its publication in the journal.

In addition to the Licence to Publish, several other instruments have been developed to protect an author's intellectual property and to facilitate the addition of scientific articles to repositories. The best known is the SPARC (Scholarly Publishing and Academic Resources Coalition) addendum (SPARC, 2006). Several (mainly American) universities have also developed an addendum, which they oblige their authors to use (Open Access Directory, 2009). From a strictly legal viewpoint, an addendum is binding only if both parties have signed it. If an author sends the addendum to the publisher and the publisher returns it unsigned, a legal vacuum can occur; which rules apply in this situation is unclear, unless advance provisions were made for such a situation in the text. If such provisions are lacking, authors may assume that they can put their version of the article in the repository of their choice, while the publisher's policy may prohibit this.

The existence of various licences and addenda leads to an obscure portfolio of rights for publishers and institutions. It is difficult to keep track of which rights belong to which party, and keeping detailed records of this is an organizational and administrative burden for both parties. In particular, publishers will not accept licences and addenda developed by institutions or funders, and will adhere to their own standards. Thus, for practical, financial and organizational reasons, accessibility of digital content to the research community will benefit from the joint development by both parties of standards which dovetail with existing practice. Such co-operation needs to be encouraged, and a conservative stance on the publishers' part is not an option.

The position of publishers

Until recently it was common practice for publishers to require authors to transfer copyright to them, for reasons that were mainly in the publishers' interests. Namely, it was easy to act against plagiarism and other copyright infringements, and the publishers' rights portfolios were orderly and provided a foundation for secondary exploitation of works. Publishing contracts were set up in such a manner that certain rights either were retained by the author or were given back by the publisher to the author. The rights falling to the author were carefully specified and comprised mainly those allowing authors to use their work in course packs, in the classroom or for future works, or to share it with colleagues. Reuse in a wider sense or for a larger user group was rarely permitted under these contracts. The rise of personal web pages and institutional repositories led to adjustments in many publishers' policies. Clauses were added to publishing contracts stating that the work could be published on the author's home page, or that a pre-print and later a post-print could be added to the repository of the author's institution. The publishing contract is slowly changing from a transfer of rights to a licence. In 2008 53% of the publishers still asked for a transfer of rights; in 2003 this was 83% (Cox and Cox, 2008).

The response to licensing initiatives

In 2008, the SURF Foundation investigated whether the Licence to Publish had been adopted by publishers (Beunen, 2007). The results of the survey showed that a number of publishers did support the underlying principles. Furthermore, the same number of publishers (16) already have a repository policy in place which is compatible with the underlying principles of the Licence to Publish. Moreover, seven publishers conform to both aspects and thus they endorse all the principles. Other publishers already used a licence, but not that developed by SURF and JISC. The same group was found to have a repository policy that accorded with the underlying principles of the Licence to Publish.

The survey did not look into why publishers did not use the Licence to Publish, although this is something that it would be interesting to know.

A possible explanation is the presence of two specific clauses in the Licence, concerning the version of the published article that is to be put in the repository and the duration of the embargo. The Licence to Publish asks for use of the PDF version produced by the publisher. This was a deliberate choice during the development of the Licence, despite the problems it might cause. Deciding on the PDF version circumvented the problems that are caused by different versions of the article and the different definitions of these versions that are used in publishing contracts. The licence fixes the duration of the embargo at six months, which is the period stipulated by many funders for the placement in subject or institutional repositories of the results of research they have financed.

Following on from its survey, the SURF Foundation, in consultation with publishers and funders, is developing an adapted version of the Licence to Publish. The aim is to introduce and promote a standard licence acceptable to all stakeholders.

The PEER project

The lack of consensus between publishers and research communities on authors' rights of self-archiving and on the duration of the embargo on publication of articles deposited in repositories was one of the reasons for the PEER (Publishing and the Ecology of European Research) project (PEER, 2009). This joint venture between publishers and the research community, subsidized by the European e-Content*plus* (European Commission, 2009) project, is looking into the effects of large-scale, systematic self-archiving of authors' manuscripts on journal viability. Among the factors being taken into consideration are the effects on reader access, author visibility and journal viability, and on the broader ecology of European research. In the PEER project, publishers, funders, authors/users and libraries/repositories are co-operating. The aim is to produce a better understanding of large-scale deposit and, through this, to inform future policies. The project also aims to produce models showing how traditional publishing can exist alongside self-archiving. Last but not least, the programme should lead to trust and mutual understanding between the parties involved.

How users can know what they can and cannot do

Authors are advised to make clear to their readers the conditions under which their work can be reused. This is not yet common practice, and many works that are being distributed as OA publications have not been provided with a user licence. Further, the majority of repositories making scholarly works available do not provide clear information to users on how they are allowed to reuse works. The absence of a user licence limits the possibilities for reuse to those legally warranted. An author can choose between different types of licence to inform users about what they are allowed to do with her work. She can use a licence as specified within the Berlin Declaration, one of the Creative Commons licences, or a different Open Content licence. Each of these licences specifies precisely what uses are allowed. Open Content licences, also called 'copyleft licences' (the practice of using copyright law to remove restrictions on distributing copies and modified versions of a work for others and requiring that the same freedoms be preserved in modified versions), operate within the boundaries of copyright, but the author owning the copyright in the work being published waives certain rights. If a user oversteps the boundaries set by the author, the regular legal copyright rules apply and the user is violating the author's rights.

Creative Commons licences

An Open Content licence does not necessarily lead to the widest distribution. The suite of Creative Commons licences illustrates this. Using a Creative Commons Public Domain licence, authors can add their work to the public domain (this licence will not be discussed here). The widest distribution of a work is provided for under a Creative Commons Attribution licence. Under this licence a work can be copied, distributed, displayed and performed, the only condition stipulated by the licence being that the user states the author's name with each use of the work. Under a Creative Commons Attribution licence, commercial use of the work and the making of derivative works are permitted. The most restrictive of the Creative Commons licences, the Creative Commons Attribution-Non-Commercial-No-Derivative-Works licence, allows only limited additional freedom as compared to the legal provisions. Under this licence, users are allowed to copy the work, distribute it and forward it, as long as they do not do so commercially. The making of derivative works under this licence is prohibited.

Within the range between these most liberal and most restrictive licences, there are four other standard licences. In each of the six varieties, users are allowed to reproduce the work under licence, include it in one or more collections and reproduce it from such collections, free of charge. In addition, they are permitted to distribute copies or audio recordings of the work, display the work publicly, present or perform it by means of a digital sound transfer, separately or as part of a collection, and retrieve and reuse it in databases. Apart from that, basic provisions apply to all varieties of the licence, stating for example that the licence is irrevocable and that it is being granted for the duration of the copyright.

To conclude, all licences contain one or more of the following provisions: permission or injunction to use the work commercially, permission or injunction to make adaptations of the work, and the obligation to include the same licence provisions when making the work available to others.

The use of Creative Commons licences has really taken off: in December 2008, worldwide there were 150 million works on the internet with a Creative Commons licence attached to them (Creative Commons, 2009). This is in part a result of the simple licensing procedures of Creative Commons. The only thing an author has to do is choose the preferred licence variety on the Creative Commons website and confirm the choice. The website then provides an HTML code for including the licence statement on web pages.

Creative Commons licence varieties are available in three versions: a simplified version for non-lawyers, a legal version (the actual licence), and a computer-readable version. In online environments the licence statement accompanying a licensed work refers to the simplified version on the Creative Commons server; this simplified version contains a reference to the actual licence. In particular, the computer-readable version has a great advantage in that it enables users to perform simple internet searches for reusable works.

Other types of Open Content licence

Other Open Content licences are less popular than Creative Commons ones. After a limited survey of the use of Open Content licences in research and education, it was concluded that a Creative Commons Attribution licence provides the best guarantee of enabling educational and research materials to be used in the ways that are advocated in education (Keller and Mossink, 2008). Other Open Content licences are less fully developed, or unsuitable for use in these specific contexts.

The licence that was made especially for OA, the Berlin Declaration licence, is hardly used at all. This licence is less suitable because it lacks the advantages of a simplified licensing procedure and a computer-readable version.

The problem of orphan works

Advancing technology, and thus the declining costs of digitization, is the key to mass digitization projects in libraries, archives and museums. This mass digitization creates new problems which hinder online availability to a bigger audience. Digitization is an act that is protected by copyright and requires the permission of the rights holder. Often the rights holder can be neither identified nor located, and in such cases we speak of an 'orphan work'. The costs and effort involved in the search for rights holders, and the copyright problems connected to orphan works, have discouraged organizations holding analogue content from digitizing it on a large scale. The average proportion of orphan works in collections across the UK's public sector has been estimated at 5% to 10%, while in certain sectors (archives) the proportion is higher (Korn, 2009).

Implications for dissemination and preservation work

Solving the problem of orphan works gained high importance with the development of the European Digital Library Europeana, the provider of a common multilingual access point to Europe's digital cultural heritage. The European Commission launched the initiative in 2005 as part of its overall strategy to boost the digital economy under the i2010 initiative (European Commission, 2005).

At an early stage, the European Commission sensed that copyright constituted an obstacle to realizing a European digital library. To establish the extent of the problem and formulate a solution, a High Level Expert Group on European Digital Libraries was set up, consisting of representatives of cultural heritage institutions and organizations of rights holders. A crucial question to be answered by this group was what different actions and arrangements could be undertaken jointly by stakeholders to reduce the tensions surrounding copyright. In June 2008 the High Level Expert Group adopted the *Final Report on Digital Preservation, Orphan Works and Out-of-Print Works*, which established the basic points of departure for digitizing cultural heritage (European Commission, 2008). Digitizing works of cultural heritage, and onsite and online use of the digitized works, are only possible with the permission of the rights holders, or should be based on the limitations and exceptions to the exclusive rights of the rights holders. Cultural heritage institutions engaged in digitizing projects derive legal certainty from this permission.

A guarantee to rights holders about the use of their works means that all rights need to be cleared on the basis of either an individual or a collective licence. For born-digital works, this implies that permission is needed for online availability, and for analogue works it implies that permission is needed to make a digital copy. Getting permission touches directly on the question of identifying the rights holder. The impossibility of finding or tracing rights holders hampers comprehensive, large-scale digitization and online access projects as well as other uses, and means that libraries, museums, archives and other non-profit institutions may be prevented from fully exploiting the benefits of information technology to carry out their preservation and dissemination mandates. Some uses of orphan works may fall within the scope of existing exceptions, but even these specific exceptions would not permit much activity involving orphan works (British Screen Advisory Council, 2006).

Approaches to a solution

Several approaches to the problem of orphan works are possible, via a legal solution or via contractual arrangements. The law provides for an orphan work to be used under certain conditions when users have proved that they cannot find the rights holder after a reasonable search. A legal solution to the problem could either include an exception in the existing copyright law or introduce a licensing system by which users obtained a licence from a government or judicial body prior to use and after demonstrating their reasonable search. Both approaches have advantages and disadvantages. An exception-based system is easy for a user and has low costs and high efficiency. The user is only required to pay a rights holder if the rights holder appears and claims a fee. The licence that is issued stipulates the terms of use and thus provides the user with legal certainty, especially when that licence is issued by a government body. A great disadvantage is that the user has first to conduct a diligent search and has to pay a licence fee even if the rights holder cannot be traced.

UK legislation currently provides for the use of a work if it is not possible by reasonable inquiry to ascertain the identity of the author and if it is reasonable to assume that the copyright has expired. Section 57 of the Copyright, Designs and Patents Act 1988 (CDPA) specifies that an infringement does not occur where the copyright owner cannot be located by a reasonable inquiry and when the date of copyright expiration must be uncertain, or when it is reasonable to assume that the copyright has expired or that the author died 70 years or more before the beginning of the calendar year in which the act of copying is done or the arrangements are made. This provision, however, will not solve the problem of orphan works, because under present law libraries and archives may make one copy of an analogue format literary, dramatic or musical work from their permanent collection, *in the same format*, in order to preserve it.

In 2005 the UK government commissioned an independent review of the CDPA to establish whether the Act was still fit for purpose in the changing economic and increasingly globalized environment of the digital age. The *Gowers Review of Intellectual Property* (HM Treasury, 2006) suggested proposals on a wide range of policy issues regarding copyright. To solve the problem of orphan works, the Review recommended that the government should propose provision for orphan works to the European Commission by amendment of the Information Society Directive, and that the UK Patent Office should issue clear guidance on the parameters of a 'reasonable search' for the copyright holders of orphan works, in consultation with stakeholders. Finally, the Review stated that the UK Patent Office should establish a voluntary register of copyright, either on its own or through partnerships with database holders.

Current European solutions

The European Commission did not opt for an exception to be introduced into the Copyright Directive (European Union, 2001), but chose an interoperable solution, to be obtained by contractual arrangements. A specially established High Level Expert Group Copyright Subgroup focused on the development of practical solutions for digital preservation, out-of-print works and orphan works. This group has six key principles, one of which is transparency. It said: 'Clarification and transparency in the copyright status of a work is an essential element in a number of areas including the European Digital

Library Initiative.' (DLHLEG, 2007). Three methods it proposed for achieving this were non-legislative solutions that enhance transparency and/or prevent the further expansion of the phenomenon of orphan works:

- dedicated databases concerned with information on orphan works
- improved inclusion of metadata – information on rights holders – in the digital material
- enhanced contractual practices, particularly for audiovisual works.

The European preference for regulating the use and reuse of orphan works without changing the corpus of EU law (the *Acquis Communautaire*) has led to arrangements between collecting societies, organizations of right holders and cultural heritage institutions. Within the scope of the Copyright Subgroup, representatives from cultural institutions and the creative sectors were invited to take part in sector-specific working groups with a mandate to create guidelines for their respective sectors for cultural institutions seeking to find rights holders of works that might be orphan. These guidelines include the criteria for a diligent search to be undertaken before digitizing a work. Each category of works has a slightly different definition of an orphan work.

An orphan work is a work that has rights holders whose permission is required to use it but who can either not be identified or not be located, based on a diligent search on the foundation of due diligence guidelines. This search must be both in good faith (subjective) and reasonable, given the type of rights holder (objective). The parties agreed on several criteria by which a work can be called 'orphan'. This is only possible if a rights holder cannot be found when the criteria for due diligence search have been followed. Considering that the standards of due diligence could best be established in collaboration between representatives of rights holders and cultural institutions, the stakeholders declared in a Memorandum of Understanding (MoU) that they had searched on a voluntary basis for generic due diligence guidelines as a practicable and flexible tool for facilitating the identification and location of rights holders for the lawful use of orphan works. In this MoU the stakeholders also undertook to promote the guidelines for diligent search as acceptable standards in dealing with orphan works across Europe, to encourage and support the further development of tools to identify and mechanisms to facilitate the lawful use of orphan works, and to advocate measures to prevent future works from becoming orphan.

The Dutch solution

Tracing and finding the copyright rights holders in order to ask for permission to digitize and reuse works places an administrative and financial burden on libraries and other cultural and/or educational organizations. This may lead to their abandoning the idea of digitization. To make digitization possible, and to make works from the collections of cultural heritage institutions in the Netherlands available, the Dutch Library Forum and the branch organization of the Dutch collecting societies for copyright and related rights have chosen contractual arrangements. They have signed a declaration to clarify matters for institutions regarding the digitization of their (heritage) collections (Digiti©E Committee, 2009). Under this declaration, it will be possible for institutions to make their collections available on their own premises for the purposes of teaching, research or private study without conducting a diligent search. However, works to be digitized by publicly accessible libraries, museums and archives must fulfil certain criteria in order to make use of these provisions. The works must form part of the Dutch cultural heritage and must have been legally acquired. Furthermore, to the best knowledge of the institution, the works to be digitized must be no longer commercially available and the rights regarding the works to be digitized must be vested in Dutch rights holders or in rights holders who can be represented by a Dutch collecting society.

The arrangement means that institutions do not need to devote an unnecessarily large amount of time and money to searching for rights holders and making arrangements regarding reuse. The collecting societies will conduct the diligent search. For further online distribution, the consent of the rights holder will remain necessary and a reasonable payment must be made. Prior to any other type of reproduction or provision of access to the works, organizations must contact a registration centre to negotiate between the rights holder and cultural heritage institution with regard both to provision of access as such and to reasonable payment.

Conclusion: vision for the future

Overall availability of scholarly information will be of utmost importance in the future. The information should be available with a single mouse click, at any time and anywhere. It should be reusable in any form or format, and data mining, text mining and sampling should be allowed. These expectations extend not only to born-digital works, but also to analogue works stored in libraries, archives and museums. These are expected to be available for researchers, teachers, students and also a wider audience. Institutions of higher education invest large amounts in the establishment and management of digital repositories and work hard to make their scholarly output as open as possible. OA, Open Content and open data are becoming part of an overall framework within universities, and the information provided by those institutions is becoming a fundamental component of public research information.

Partnerships and governance structures

As demonstrated earlier, to achieve the goal of the broadest availability of scholarly output, co-operation between the stakeholders is very important. With regard to digitization, online accessibility and digital preservation of Europe's collective memory, Europe has introduced another form of co-operation between the parties involved, which operates within the framework of applicable copyright and intellectual property law. According to the European Commission, public-private partnerships can play an important role in Europe's efforts to digitize its cultural heritage. Private partners can bring to the table the funding, technology, software and expertise required for large-scale digitization. By combining this with the experience in resource discovery and user requirements of cultural-heritage institutions, public access to collections can be enhanced. However, public–private partnerships involve some risks. Such partnerships must be managed very carefully to prevent them from ending in failure and the material to be digitized thus never becoming available for access on reasonable terms. The allocation of ownership of copyright and of other applicable intellectual property rights after digitization needs to be clearly stated. Furthermore, to be successful, several other starting points need to be taken into account.

There is a need for a formal, transparent, accountable partnership managed through a formal governance structure which does not establish exclusive agreements that are not time limited. The vision, mission and strategic objectives of all partners and the public benefits to be achieved through the project must be clearly laid out. Finally, the sustainability of the business model for the long term is very important.

Legal reform in Europe on the problem of orphan works will prove to be very difficult. Each member state will have to implement the new provisions, and heavy lobbying will probably not lead to a desirable situation.

Co-operation between publishers, libraries and authors

In the larger area of scholarly communication, stakeholders working together need to guarantee the broadest availability of scholarly output. Publishers, libraries and authors should value the contributions of each stakeholder and regard scholarly communication as part of the infrastructure of a global edifice of scholarship. All stakeholders need to aim towards forward thinking. Because of the long debates, the positions of the diverse parties involved in the copyright arrangement have moved slightly. Any forward movement cannot be expected from legal reform, because the position between libraries, authors and publishers is regulated mainly by contract law and not by copyright or intellectual property rights. With regard to ownership of content, the positions of universities and authors are laid out in law, but the way in which universities have interpreted the provisions has clouded, rather than clarified, subsequent positions. It seems that a status quo has been reached with regard to the ownership of digital content. Further clarification between the stakeholders about the bundle of rights involved in copyright may be possible by formulating policies and licences that are acceptable to all parties involved. The rights to preserve the material and to access this preserved material may be a new point for discussion, as institutions of higher education and libraries are addressing this issue more and more. Probably, publishing agreements will develop along the route of path-dependence: the set of decisions one faces for any given circumstance is limited by the decisions one has made in the past, even though past circumstances may no longer be relevant (Monotti and Ricketson, 2003).

Another practice which may be questioned in the future is the existing one of depositing the final version of the author's manuscript accepted for publication in a scientific journal. With the emergence of the data deluge, the emphasis will be not only on the publication, but also on the underlying resources. Stakeholders should make arrangements for data storage, data mining and text mining, not only in publishing agreements but also in the licence agreements for electronic scientific journals.

One last question might be raised. Despite the growth of Open Content and OA, journals are still the mainstay of scholarly communication, but speed of publication is often mentioned as being the big advantage of repositories. Peers are informed about the latest state of the art mainly via the deposit of a pre-print in the repository. In addition to scholarly output deposited in a repository, articles are available through institutions' journal subscriptions. Universities put a lot of organizational and financial effort into making available the same journal articles that are already available through journal subscriptions. Such availability of the content could be an argument for evaluating decisions about which scholarly output is deposited in a repository. Would it not make more sense to consider, together with the publishers' community, whether it might be possible to deposit other material in the repository, and to define new arrangements in such a manner that scholarly output partly owned by the publishers will become more broadly available for a larger audience?

Notes

1   Dame Lynne Brindley, response to the Gowers Review.

2   www.teleread.org/2009/09/01/10-most-pirated-ebooks-not-what-you-think/.

3   http://in.answers.yahoo.com/question/index?qid=20090801080757AAMcIFt.

4   UK Copyright, Designs and Patents Act 1988, Section 11 (1), Chapter 48.

5   Copyright Law of the United States and Related Rights Contained in Title 17 of the United States Code: Originality, fixation in a tangle medium, § 201.

6   Community for Creative Non-Violence vs Reid, 490 U.S. 730 (1989); see http://caselaw.lp.findlaw.com/scripts/getcase.pl?navby=search&court=US&case=/us/490/730.html [accessed October 2009].

7   Hays v. Sony Corp. of America, 847 F.2d 412 (7th Cir. 1988).

References

Beunen, A. (2007) *Acceptance of the JISC/SURF Licence to Publish and Accompanying Principles by Traditional Publishers of Journals*, SURF Foundation, www.surffoundation.nl/SFDocuments/LtP-final-report-dec07.pdf [accessed October 2009].

British Library (2008) Results of the British Library Copyright Questionnaire, www.bl.uk/ip/pdf/resultscopyrightquestionnaire.pdf [accessed 6 November 2009].

British Screen Advisory Council (2006) *Implementing the Gowers Review of Intellectual Property: orphan works*, British Screen Advisory Council, www.bsac.uk.com/files/IMPLEMENTING_THE_GOWERS_REVIEW_ ORPHAN_WORKS.pdf [accessed October 2009].

CETUS (Consortium for Educational Technology for University Systems) (undated) *Ownership of New Works at the University: unbundling of rights and the pursuit of higher learning*, California State University, www.eric.ed.gov/ERICWebPortal/custom/portlets/recordDetails/detailmini.jsp?_ nfpb=true&_&ERICExtSearch_SearchValue_0=ED451734&ERICExtSearch_ SearchType_0=no&accno=ED451734 [accessed October 2009].

Cox, J. and Cox, L. (2008) *Scholarly Publishing Practice, Third Survey 2008: academic journal publishers' policies and practices in online publishing*, Association of Learned and Professional Society Publishers.

Crawford, W. (2008) Library Access to Scholarship: Harvard and institutional repositories, *Cites & Insights*, **8** (4), http://citesandinsights.info/v8i4b.htm [accessed October 2009].

Creative Commons (2009) *Metrics*, http://wiki.creativecommons.org/Metrics [accessed October 2009].

Crews, K. and Wong, D. (2004) *Ownership and Rights of Use of Works Created at the University: a survey of American university copyright policies*, Copyright Management Center, http://copyright.surf.nl/copyright/files/Policy_analysis_ownership_zwolleIII.pdf [accessed October 2009].

Crews, K. D. and van Westrienen, G. (2007) Copyright, Publishing and Scholarship: the 'Zwolle Group' Initiative for the Advance of Higher Education, *D-Lib Magazine*, **13** (1/2), www.dlib.org/dlib/january07/crews/01crews.html [accessed October 2009].

Davenport, E. (1994) Perceptions of Copyright in a Group of UK Information Scientists, *ASLIB Proceedings*, **46** (11), 267–74.

Digiti©E Committee (2009) *Declaration by the Digiti©E Committee (Digitalisation of Cultural Heritage Collections)*,
www.sitegenerator.bibliotheek.nl/fobid/img/docs/
Declaration%20digitace%20committee.doc.

DLHLEG (2007) Digital Libraries High Level Expert Group – Copyright Subgroup, *Report on Digital Preservation, Orphan Works, and Out-of-Print Works: selected implementation issues (adopted by the High Level Expert Group at its third meeting on 18.4.2007)*.

EPrints (2009) *ROARMAP (Registry of Open Access Repository Material Archiving Policies)*, www.eprints.org/openaccess/policysignup/ [accessed October 2009].

European Commission (2005) *i2010: Digital Libraries Initiative*,
http://europa.eu/legislation_summaries/information_society/l24226i_en.htm.

European Commission (2008) High Level Expert Group – Copyright Subgroup, *Final Report on Digital Preservation, Orphan Works and Out-of-print Works*,
http://ec.europa.eu/information_society/activities/digital_libraries/doc/hleg/
reports/copyright/copyright_subgroup_final_report_26508-clean171.pdf
[accessed October 2009].

European Commission (2009) eContent*plus* – *ICT-PSP*,
http://ec.europa.eu/information_society/activities/econtentplus/index_en.htm
[accessed October 2009].

European Union (2001) Directive 2001/29/EC of the European Parliament and of the Council of 22 May 2001 on the harmonisation of certain aspects of copyright and related rights in the information society, *Official Journal of the European Communities*, 26 June, L167/10,
http://eur-lex.europa.eu/pri/en/oj/dat/2001/l_167/
l_16720010622en00100019.pdf.

Google Books (2009) *Google Books Library Project: an enhanced card catalog of the world's books*,
http://books.google.com/googlebooks/library.html [accessed October 2009].

Harvey, J. (2003) What Does Zwolle Stand For? *Learned Publishing*, 16 (4), 290–2.

Helft, M. (2009) Google's Plan for Out-of-Print Books is Challenged, *New York Times*, 4 April,
www.nytimes.com/2009/04/04/technology/internet/04books.html?_r=1.

HM Treasury (2006) *Gowers Review of Intellectual Property*,
http://webarchive.nationalarchives.gov.uk/+/www.hm-treasury.gov.uk/d/
ptr06_gowersreport_755.pdf [accessed 6 November 2009].

Intellectual Property Task Force (1999) *Intellectual Property and New Media Technologies: a framework for policy development at AAU institutions*, report to the

AAU Digital Networks and Intellectual Property Management Committee, Association of American Universities, www.aau.edu/reports/IPReport.pdf [accessed October 2009].

Keller, P. and Mossink, M. (2008) *Reuse of Material in the Context of Education and Research*, SURF Foundation, www.surffoundation.nl/en/publicaties/Pages/Reuseofmaterial.aspx [accessed October 2009].

Korn, N. (2009) *In from the Cold: an assessment of the scope of 'Orphan Works' and its impact on the delivery of services*, JISC Collections, www.jisc.ac.uk/media/documents/publications/infromthecoldv1.pdf [accessed October 2009].

Law, D. G., Weedon, R. L., and Sheen, M. R. (2000) Universities and Article Copyright, *Learned Publishing*, 13 (3), 142–50.

Lohman, F. (2008) *Google Book Search Settlement: a reader's guide*, Electronic Frontier Foundation, www.eff.org/deeplinks/2008/10/google-books-settlement-readers-guide [accessed October 2009].

Max Planck Gesellschaft (2003) *Berlin Declaration on Open Access to Knowledge in the Sciences and Humanities*, http://oa.mpg.de/openaccess-berlin/berlindeclaration.html [accessed October 2009].

Max Planck Gesellschaft (2009) *Extended Table of Signatories*, http://oa.mpg.de/openaccess-berlin/signatories.html [accessed October 2009].

McSherry, C. (2001) *Who Owns Academic Work? Battling for control of intellectual property*, Harvard University Press.

Monotti, A. L. and Ricketson, S. (2003) *Universities and Intellectual Property: ownership and exploitation*, Oxford University Press Inc.

Morris, S. (2009) *Journal Authors' Rights: perception and reality*, Publishers' Research Consortium, Summary Paper 5, www.publishingresearch.net/documents/JournalAuthorsRights.pdf [accessed October 2009].

Mossink, W. (1999) *Auteursrechten op Wetenschappelijke Publicaties*, Utrecht: Stichting SURF/IWI-Open Universiteit Nederland [in Dutch].

Open Access Directory (2009) *Author Addenda*, http://oad.simmons.edu/oadwiki/Author_addenda [accessed October 2009].

PEER (2009) *Publishing and the Ecology of European Research*, www.peerproject.eu [accessed October 2009].

Pounder, R. (2008) Peter Murray-Rust and the Data-mining Robots, ComputerWeekly.com, www.computerweekly.com/Articles/2008/02/05/229273/peter-murray-rust-and -the-data-mining-robots.htm.

SHERPA (2006) *SHERPA/RoMEO: publishers' copyright policies and self-archiving*, www.sherpa.ac.uk/projects/sherparomeo.html [accessed October 2009].

SPARC (2006) *Author Rights: using the SPARC author addendum to secure your rights as the author of a journal article*, www.arl.org/sparc/author/addendum.html [accessed October 2009].

Suber, P. (2008) The Open Access Mandate at Harvard, *SPARC Open Access Newsletter*, 119, www.earlham.edu/~peters/fos/newsletter/03-02-08.htm [accessed October 2009].

SURF Foundation (2006) *Copyright Management by Scholarship: the Zwolle Principles*, http://copyright.surf.nl/copyright/zwolle_principles.php [accessed October 2009].

SURF Foundation (undated) *JISC/SURF Copyright Toolbox*, http://copyrighttoolbox.surf.nl/copyrighttoolbox/ [accessed October 2009].

Vaidhyanathan, S. (2001) *Copyrights and Copywrongs: the rise of intellectual property and how it threatens creativity*, New York University Press.

Weedon, R. (2000) *Policy Approaches to Copyright in HEIs*, study for the JISC Committee on Awareness, Liaison and Training, Centre for Educational Systems, University of Strathclyde, www.learningservices.strath.ac.uk/docs/JCALT.pdf [accessed October 2009].

Weedon, R. and Mossink, W. (2006) *Report on Institutional Copyright Policies in the Netherlands and the UK: lessons learnt, good practices and guidelines*, SURF Foundation and JISC.

Wiseman, L. (1999) *Copyright in Universities*, Occasional Paper Series, 99-E, Australian Department of Education, Training and Youth Affairs, http://nla.gov.au/nla.cat-vn356140 [accessed October 2009].

Index